# A Joyful Noise

## A MONASTIC APPROACH TO THE PSALMS

### WILLIAM MENINGER, OCSO

Paulist Press
New York/Mahwah, NJ

Cover and book design by Sharyn Banks

Library of Congress Cataloging-in-Publication Data

Meninger, William.
    A joyful noise : a monastic approach to the Psalms / William Meninger.
        p. cm.
    ISBN 978-0-8091-4687-1 (alk. paper)
1. Bible. O.T. Psalms—Meditations. I. Title.
    BS1430.54.M46 2010
    242'.5—dc22

                                                            2010022135

Published by Paulist Press
997 Macarthur Boulevard
Mahwah, New Jersey 07430
www.paulistpress.com

Printed and bound in the
United States of America

# CONTENTS

∽

# INTRODUCTION

 ⁓

As part of the inspired Scriptures, the psalms are the words of God. They are intended by God to also be the words of men and women. This is why they are given to us in the form of hymns, prayers, and reflections. Because they are intended for human beings, they reflect the entire gamut of human emotions: aspirations, desires, hopes, regrets, fear, anger, dreams, and poetic expressions.

In the form in which they were eventually written down and collected into a single book of the Hebrew Scriptures, the psalms are inspired by God. They are an expression of the self-revelation of God, objectified and concretized as a part of the Sacred Scriptures, and accepted by God's holy people as such. However, there is another side to them. The psalms are coauthored by God and by men and women who experienced, over a period of 1,300 years, the emotions, desires, traumas, and ecstasies expressed in them. These men and women wrote them down finally as prayers or meditations to be shared by others on a personal level and in the context of communal celebrations and liturgical worship. Thus, the psalms are both human and divine in their origin, their content, and in their present-day expression.

To pray or just to read the psalms is to go on a journey. The guide for the journey is the real author of the psalms, the Holy Spirit. This book is also intended to help you on the journey. It is both personal and emotional. We are going to look at the psalms as reproducible personal religious experiences. The psalms will become our prayers, our meditations, and our expressions of our own daily experiences. Jews and Christians have always seen the psalms as poetic prayers embracing every aspect of human life. We will discover in them every emotion, every kind of trial and suffering, and every attitude toward God, self, and neighbor: from compassion, desolation, sorrow, and grief to thanksgiving, joy, and elation. There are psalms appropriate for us no matter where we are, how we feel, what we have done, or what has been done to us. Our minds, our emotions, our instinctual responses, our deeds: all have counterparts in the Psalter. There is a psalm for us to pray and to think about for every event and experience in our lives. The psalms are inspired and ultimately authored by the Holy Spirit in cooperation with dozens of singers, poets, soldiers, merchants, travelers, wise men and women, priests, prophets, and kings. We will be surprised, delighted, and, at the same time, dismayed by their relevance to our own life. We are to make them our own. We must allow the presence of that same Holy Spirit to resonate within us—and to call forth God's praise, to marvel at his awesome deeds, to beg his forgiveness, and even to question his wisdom and providence. But we will, above all, acknowledge his steadfast love.

Up until the twentieth century, when commentators wrote about the psalms, they used many different ways to classify them or to put them into categories. Most of these ways were imaginative guesswork, sometimes helpful, sometimes not. For centuries, seven of the psalms have been called the penitential psalms because they speak of sorrow for sins. Others have been classed together as creation psalms, nature psalms, joyful psalms, or sad psalms, because of their content.

Scholarly research in the twentieth century, however, has come up with a new way of classifying them. By serious study, language analysis, and an examination of content, we can classify the psalms in accordance with the reasons for which they were written and the purpose for which they were used in the worship of God's people, especially in the Temple. Thus, for example, we have the psalms of thanksgiving, sung at the Temple in gratitude for God's favors; the psalms of ascent, recited on the three yearly pilgrimages going up to Jerusalem; and the royal psalms, recited by the king on special public celebrations or times of impending calamity. We also have the wisdom psalms, intended for instruction in political or priestly duties.

As we journey through the Psalter, especially when we use the literal approach, we will include these helpful classifications. This will not be, however, our primary approach. We are interested, as I will repeat again and again, in the psalms as reproducible experiences, as divinely inspired witnesses to the events of our own daily lives. We shall find ourselves using classifications or groupings of the psalms coming from our personal needs and recognition of those particular reproducible experiences we discover in them. This is indeed more like the ancient usage of the early church, more like the practice of the traditional holy men and women of Christian history, who recognized in the psalms their own lives. So our classifications will also be based on personal compatibility with a particular psalm, due to similar experiences, attitudes, needs, and feelings. What a great way to make the psalms our own!

It is worth noting here that the most common type of psalm is called the lamentation. These may be individual, that is, recited on one's own personal behalf, or collective, that is, recited on behalf of the community or the nation. This is not surprising, as we know that most prayers being offered to God at any time are prayers of petition stemming from distressful situations. This is precisely what the lamentation psalms are for. Often these psalms express the distress of the individual or the community in terms of an actual ritual cursing of enemies. We will deal with these individually as we come across them.

The place of the psalms in the Divine Office (or Liturgy of the Hours) of the Church is the strongest witness to their divine and human nature. The Office is the official prayer of the Church and for almost 2000 years it has been recited, chanted, or read daily by uncounted millions of monks, nuns, deacons, priests, religious, and many of the laity. The most popular form of the Divine Office, as found in the fifth-century Rule of St. Benedict, requires that the Psalter be sung in its entirety once a week and makes reference to the earlier desert monks who recited it once a day.

As the official prayer of the Church, the Office is acknowledged as the voice of Christ praising the Father under the loving impulse of the Holy Spirit. There is an unending flow of praise going forth from the minds, hearts, and voices of men and women of the Church, as they gather as often as seven times a day, from the rising of the sun to its setting, manifesting the constant interaction of the human and the Divine.

We should also remember that the psalms were the official prayers of the Temple in Old Testament worship and are still recited today in synagogues all over the world. It is obvious, then, that praying the Psalter is also a profound statement of ecumenical unity among Christian churches and with Judaism. Just from a personal point of view, I have been praying the Divine Office for fifty-two years. Completing the entire Psalter at least once a week (actually much more than that!), I have recited it over 2,704 times. This does not even take into account the use of the psalms at Mass or in other liturgical prayer forms. What a joy and privilege it has been to be a part of that myriad host of faithful hearts sending forth their joyful songs to God!

The purpose of this book is to celebrate the Psalter, to enjoy and enhance the individual psalms, and to sum up the praise of God's people with the full orchestration of human voices as celebrated in the last psalm of the Psalter, Psalm 150.

Praise the LORD!
Praise God in his sanctuary;
    praise him in his mighty firmament!
Praise him for his mighty deeds;
    praise him according to his surpassing greatness!

Praise him with trumpet sound;
    praise him with lute and harp!
Praise him with tambourine and dance;
    praise him with strings and pipe!
Praise him with clanging cymbals;
    praise him with loud clashing cymbals!
Let everything that breathes praise the LORD!
Praise the LORD!

This book is intended to provide an accompaniment to a reading (praying!) of the psalms. The NRSV is used but any translation is appropriate. The Psalter is divided into five books. It is a somewhat artificial division, probably in imitation of the five books of the Torah. The first book comprises psalms 1 to 41, the second book comprises psalms 42 to 72, the third comprises psalms 73 to 89, the fourth comprises 90 to 106 and the fifth book comprises 107 to 150.

The traditional monastic approach to interpreting the Scriptures allows us to approach it from three levels of meaning. The first level is the literal meaning, that is, what the author of the psalm actually intended. The second level is called the christological meaning, that is, how the text can be applied to Christ or his Church. This approach is used especially with texts from the Old Testament with the understanding that all of the Old Testament is directed toward preparing for Jesus and his kingdom. The third level is called the moral meaning, that is, how the text may be applied to the individual reading it. Sometimes the commentaries use one of these levels, or two, or even all three. The reader is encouraged to make personal applications of the psalms in accordance with these levels of understanding. This commentary on the psalms can be useful for *lectio divina*, that is, prayer and meditation: by first, reading the psalm, then by reading the commentary, and then slowly and prayerfully by repeating the psalm.

# BOOK ONE

# PSALMS
# I TO 4I

# PSALM 1

*Happy are those whose delight is in the law of the LORD.*

∾

This is our invitation to the Book of Psalms. We are given a choice: either the way of sinners or the way of the righteous; either the fruitfulness of a tree planted by flowing streams or the barrenness of chaff driven away by the wind. Each of the 150 psalms of the Psalter repeats, in its own way, these options. Each one is an opportunity to reaffirm our commitment to God and to be blessed (to be happy!) or to be the cause of our own sorrow. Keeping the Law of the Lord (Torah) is much more than some legalistic grasping of do's and don'ts. It is to walk in the light of God's will, to stand in the congregation of the righteous, and to be recognized by the Lord.

We walk, we stand, and we sit in the way of the Lord. His law embraces every facet of our lives. The way of the wicked will perish. They will be the cause of their own downfall. There is a warning here to make the way of the righteous our own pathway. Prosperity—true happiness—will be ours when we delight in God's law day and night. Pray Psalm 1! It is a beautiful and powerful entrance into the way of the Lord and his kingdom.

# PSALM 2

*Happy are all who take refuge in him.*

∾

To walk in the way of the righteous is not an easy thing. No man is an island, and we are all inextricably bound by our interconnectedness. Our choices are influenced and even, at times, determined by politics, economics, national and international social pressures, wars, and famines. We are subject to global movements beyond our control, and these are often determined by the amoral, economic greed of corporations, totalitarian governments, or ambitious politicians. These are the kings of the earth, who set themselves against the Lord and his Christ.

To pray Psalm 2 is to grasp the hope offered us by a loving God. He laughs at the foibles of self-willed dictators, power-mad politicians, uncontrolled military forces, terrorists, and unscrupulous businessmen. He has sent us his Son and given him the ends of the earth as his kingdom. We are all invited to take refuge in him and to experience the hope God promises, which is more powerful than the conspiracies of nations and the vain plotting of their rulers. Victory will be ours.

# PSALM 3

*But you, O LORD, are a shield around me, my glory,
and the one who lifts up my head.*

∽

"Oh LORD, how many are my foes!" The opening verse of this psalm says it all—or does it? Certainly there are days when we feel like this. It can seem as if 10,000 people have set themselves against us. But we know that this is not the last word. Indeed, our strength arises from our weakness. We know the Lord sustains us and we are not afraid.

Can we consent to this prayer that the Lord will strike the cheeks of our enemies and break the teeth of the wicked? This reflects the Old Testament mentality of "an eye for an eye," and we realize that it is no longer valid. Whenever we see these or similar verses from the so-called "cursing psalms," we must be guided by the new teaching of Jesus: "You have heard that it was said, 'You shall love your neighbor and hate your enemy.' But I say to you, Love your enemies and pray for those who persecute you" (Matt 5:43–44). Let the cursing psalms remind us that we live under a new commandment and that the Lord has made all things new.

# PSALM 4

*I will both lie down and sleep in peace; for you alone,*
*O LORD, make me lie down in safety.*

∼

This is a prayer appropriately said in the evening before retiring. Perhaps it has not been a good day, and the psalmist has unjustly been subject to lies and accusations. He does not lament or curse his enemies, because his trust in the Lord is so strong. While he may feel irritation and anger, he does not allow it to spill over into rash action or even to disturb his sleep. He knows what he is called to do and what sacrifices are required of him, and he even rejoices because he is assured of God's blessings. They will be even more wonderful than mere material prosperity, better then abundant crops of grain or harvest of grapes. What beautiful words to utter as one retires for the night: "I will both lie down and sleep in peace, for you alone, O LORD, make me lie down in safety." By praying Psalm 4, we give utterance to the voice of Christ and to all the members of his body who suffer persecution for justice's sake!

# PSALM 5

*O LORD, in the morning you hear my voice.*

∾

If Psalm 4 is to be said before going to bed, then Psalm 5, with some reservations, is to be said the next morning. Psalm 5 combines lament, cursing, and trust: "LORD, give heed to my sighing....You hate all evildoers....Let all who take refuge in you rejoice; let them ever sing for joy."

However, the best way to get rid of your enemies is to make them your friends. This is the solution that Jesus offers: "I say to you, Do not resist an evildoer. But if anyone strikes you on the right cheek, turn the other also; and if anyone wants to sue you and take your coat, give him your cloak as well" (Matt 5:39–40). So do not curse but pray for your enemies. God does not delight in wickedness, and evildoers may not dwell with him. So pray for them that they too might worship toward God's holy temple, take refuge in the Lord, and ever sing for joy.

# PSALM 6

*Turn, O LORD, save my life; deliver me for*
*the sake of your steadfast love.*

∾

There are times when we simply need to moan and groan. Psalm 6 provides us with that opportunity. It is not a useless, unheeded lamentation: our crying is directed to the Lord who hears our weeping and accepts it as our prayer. We should pray this psalm even at times when we are not overwhelmed with affliction, because all of our prayers are corporate; that is, they are more than personal pleas but issue forth from the entire Body of Christ. We should speak these words for all who are oppressed and, especially, for those burdened by troubles who do not know or trust in God. The psalms go forth at all times and for all the Church. There are always those who are bowed down by grief, illness, or betrayal; that is, by enemies. Even when we are temporarily freed from most of these ills, it is good for us to think of and pray for others not as fortunate. We make their pleas our own even as we echo the voice of Jesus in the Garden of Gethsemane: "Father, if you are willing, remove this cup from me; yet, not my will but yours be done" (Luke 22:42).

# PSALM 7

*God is my shield, who saves the upright in heart.*

In this psalm we contend with God in much the way that Job did. What have I done to be treated so harshly? Let God call an assembly and preside over my trial. Then I will be seen to be innocent and will be judged according to my righteousness! But is any one of us so innocent? Are we not all sinners who have done what is evil in God's sight? This psalm can be prayed quite literally by all those who put their trust in the Lord because they has been vindicated by Christ who has won the victory for them and, by this psalm, are reaching out to claim that victory. We are given the innocence of the Lamb of God, and our shield is God who saves the upright of heart. It is not my righteousness that saves me, but God's. And I will give him thanks for it.

My enemies are those who "conceive evil, and are pregnant with mischief, and bring forth lies." They dig a pit and fall into it themselves. Their violence descends upon their own heads. As for me, I will thank and praise the Lord!

# PSALM 8

*You have set your glory above the heavens.*

∽

When this beautiful psalm of praise was written, the psalmist had before him the creation accounts of the first two chapters of Genesis. He begins and ends with an antiphon or refrain declaring the greatness of God's majesty in all the earth. All creation sings of the glory of God. The psalmist gazes up into the night sky and sees the moon and the stars, which the fingers of God have flung across the firmament. He is awestruck by the fact that the great God of this incredible creation has given it to us so that we have dominion over all the works of God's hands. Just as God sits enthroned above the heavens, with the world as his footstool, so do men and women rule over it all subject only to God.

When we pray this psalm we acknowledge on behalf of all creation—plants, animals, birds, oceans, and stars—the greatness of God. We give them a voice. When we accept this role of dominion, we also accept its responsibilities: to enable all creatures to increase and multiply, and to allow the earth to sing forth the praises of God. The environment is ours to enjoy and also to re-create so that it may continue to reflect the beauty, the fecundity, and the majesty of God. To pray this psalm is to make a commitment to a green earth!

# PSALM 9

*Sing praises to the LORD, who dwells in Zion.*
*Declare his deeds among the peoples.*

∽

Psalms 9 and 10 are really only one psalm and are found as one in the oldest manuscripts. This single psalm incorporates three types of Hebrew poetry and was edited in its final form rather late, perhaps around 250 BC. It is a psalm of praise, a lamentation psalm, and a wisdom psalm. As a psalm of praise, it gives thanks to God for the wonderful things he has done for the psalmist. As a lamentation psalm, it takes on the reproaches of the cursing psalms. As a wisdom psalm, it is an acrostic; that is, each line begins with a different letter of the Hebrew alphabet. This symbolically states that the psalm says everything it needs to say, that the psalm says all that can be said through the medium of words. We will treat this single psalm as two, as it is currently edited, and see how we can make both of them our own prayer.

Psalm 9 praises God for all his wonderful deeds. Usually, this refers to miracles for the purpose of delivering the Israelites from Egypt and leading them to the Promised Land. Wonderful deeds, then, usually refer to God's gracious dealings with the nation, the people as a whole. Here God's mercy to the psalmist is equated with his mercy to the whole people. Enemies of the psalmist are enemies of God's people and enemies of God. This is true even when those enemies are themselves from the people.

God is a righteous judge and he has exonerated the psalmist through the justice system of the Temple, which embodies his just judgments. He will also mete out justice to his enemies. This judgment will be executed by the enemies themselves, as they are trapped in the evil works of their own hands. Perhaps this is less a curse than a moral statement: evildoers are eventually caught up in their own malice.

As Christians, we are called to reverse this ordering of things. We even make the evil deeds of our enemies occasions of praying for them for their conversions, thus advancing even further the wonderful works of God. They will be judged, but in the light of Christ's mercy and the prayers of the persecuted.

# PSALM 10

*Rise up, O LORD,...lift up your hand;*
*do not forget the oppressed.*

∽

Psalm 10 is the voice of God giving utterance to the cries of the poor, the persecuted, the downtrodden, and the suffering all over the world. It is the voice of Christ on the cross, the cry of Job on his dung heap. It pierces the heavens, coming directly from the hearts of men and women who have nothing left to hold up before God except their misery and helplessness. If there is anything of joy left for these people, it is smothered by their daily wretchedness and the denials of their God-given rights to "life, liberty, and the pursuit of happiness."

It is all the worse when their afflictions convince them that God has hidden his face. He is like a father who does not respond to the needs of his children. Those responsible for their misery flourish with impunity. They mock God and even deny his existence. They hide behind their prosperity, which they do not perceive as even being threatened.

We must add our voices to the cry of our suffering brothers and sisters and let our outrage and our prayers strengthen their hope. "O LORD, you will hear the desire of the meek; you will strengthen their heart, you will incline your ear." Let this psalm remind us that there are such people subsisting in our world and that God often depends on us to give them voice and to be his instruments in coming to their aid.

# PSALM 11

*For the LORD is righteous; he loves righteous deeds;*
*the upright shall behold his face.*

∽

This is a wonderful psalm of trust. Other psalms of trust are Psalms 16, 23, and 27. The very opening line (found also in a dozen other psalms) says it all. "In the LORD I take refuge." The psalmist has been counseled to flee from his persecutors "like a bird to the mountains." He refuses. He shares with us the hope that the Holy Spirit has placed in his heart so that it becomes our prayer, one that can be repeated many times a day and that can bring comfort and trust each time we say it: "In the LORD I take refuge."

We live in a moral universe. The Lord, whose throne is in heaven, is also in his holy Temple and rules over all. We see daily the foundations of civilization threatened by war, terrorism, greed, and a lack of faith. The Lord is not indifferent to these things. His eyes behold, he tests the righteous and the wicked, and we are reassured that the upright shall look upon his face.

# PSALM 12

*You, O LORD, will protect us.*

∽

It almost seems as if the author of Psalm 12 reads our newspapers and watches our daily evening news on television! Is there anyone left with some sense of morality, responsibility, or public service? Who can be believed or trusted? Hope is found in an oracle, possibly from Isaiah. It expresses the immediacy, the determination, and the strength of the Lord's response to the groans of the needy. "I will now rise up," says the Lord. His word is a word of power. Unlike lies from the flattering lips of deceivers, God's promises have the strength and beauty of pure, refined silver. He will protect us.

This psalm belongs to the wisdom literature and expresses the mature reflection of the wise man. By praying it, we can willingly become partakers of that maturity and wisdom. St. James, who experienced the glory of God's word, was very conscious of the evil that could come from the tongue. "For every species of beast and bird, of reptile and sea creature, can be tamed and has been tamed by the human species, but no one can tame the tongue—a restless evil, full of deadly poison" (James 3:7–8). We can trust in the Lord whose word is truth.

# PSALM 13

*But I trusted in your steadfast love; my heart shall
rejoice in your salvation.*

∽

The psalms provide us with the opportunity to confront, examine, and let go of the entire gamut of human emotions. In them we will find room for our every desire, regret, and hope. The answer will always be God: the bottom line, trusting God; the attraction, God's merciful love; the comfort, God's all-embracing forgiveness; the hope, to dwell in the house of God forever.

Psalm 13 follows the classic pattern for a personal lament with its threefold structure:

1. The lament or complaint

2. The appeal to God

3. Confidence in God's loving response

It is good for us to openly and honestly place before God our pain and sorrow. Indeed it is our distress that prompts us to turn to God in prayer and with a confession of our helplessness. The answer comes from our faith in God, our experience of past grace, and our confidence in his promises. It is impossible to read this poignantly beautiful psalm without identifying with its sentiments.

# PSALM 14

*The LORD looks down from heaven. . .to see if there*
*are any who are wise, who seek after God.*

≈

In several ways, this psalm is reminiscent of the way of speaking and teaching of the prophets. It sounds very much like passages in Isaiah and Jeremiah where the ruling classes are called to account for their apostasy. The fool who says in his heart, "There is no God," is neither an atheist nor a simpleton. Rather, this refers to someone who lives as though there is no God. It refers to the corrupt and to the doers of abominable deeds. They are the opposite of the wise men who are seekers of God. Someone has said that people who worry are, on a practical level, atheists. The psalmist here is saying that people who do not observe the Law of God are the actual atheists and fools.

Every Christian would do well to apply this psalm and its admonitions to his or her own personal life. How many people who sit in our churches on a Sunday morning are practical atheists? It is not for us to accuse them of hypocrisy but rather to look into our own hearts. Do we have the right understanding of a practical Christianity? Do we cry out, "Lord, Lord," in our prayers while at the same time depriving others of their rights to, at least, frugal comfort?

# PSALM 15

*Who may dwell on your holy hill?*

〰

This is a didactic or teaching psalm. Such psalms were written rather late in the history of Israel and are similar to the wisdom psalms. The opening verse, "O LORD, who may abide in your tent?" should be taken quite literally. It is a kind of examination of conscience in preparation for a visit to the Temple, possibly to ask the priest for an oracle or prophecy to guide the psalmist before he writes.

It is not concerned with liturgical rules or dietary restrictions but rather with the social bonds of fraternal relationships so necessary for the well-being of the community. References are made to laws from the Torah. These laws, as principles of morality, are as valid today as they were when the psalm was written. There are ten requirements that must be observed before a visit to the Temple, modeled, no doubt, on the Ten Commandments. When we pray this psalm today, we must also consider the two great commandments—love of God and love of neighbor, also found in the Torah—as requirements for placing ourselves in the presence of God, who dwells no longer in the Temple but in the hearts of his people, in the Body of his Christ.

# PSALM 16

*You are my LORD; I have no good apart from you.*

∽

This is a psalm of trust. It differs from the lamentation psalms in that God is approached, not as one who has been absent, but as one present and actively supporting and protecting the psalmist. "Protect me, O God....I have no good apart from you." This will find its fullest expression in the words of Jesus: "For what will it profit them if they gain the whole world but forfeit their life?" (Matt 16:26).

In the night, a time favorable for divine counsel, the Lord instructs the wise heart. The whole man is the object of God's blessing: "My heart is glad, and my soul rejoices; my body also rests secure." Thus, the whole man is enabled to observe the first great commandment to "love the Lord with your whole mind and heart, body and soul." The right path taken by the just man in Psalm 1 is made clear by the guidance of God.

# PSALM 17

*I call upon you, for you will answer me, O God;*
*incline your ear to me.*

◦◦◦

This is yet another lamentation psalm, but when we pray it, we must see any person, thing, or situation that would move us away from God as our enemies. Can we honestly make such a case for our innocence? Can we honestly say that there is no wickedness in us, that not our hearts nor our mouths nor our feet have transgressed? If we let Christ be our mediator and hear him praying this psalm on our behalf, then we can proclaim our innocence!

To say that my cause is just and my lips are free from deceit is hardly the prayer Jesus urges us to say. "O Lord, be merciful to me, a sinner" is closer to our reality. Yet we can make a claim to his righteousness and his obedience to the Father. Jesus continues to be crucified in all the suffering people in the world. Let us join in their cry that God will protect us under the shelter of his wing.

We should take literally the last four verses where a curse is given in the form of a blessing. Let us pray earnestly for our enemies and for their children. The psalmist is not referring to life after death when he says he will "behold God's face in righteousness," but for us, it can express our confidence in God's promise of a place where there shall be no more mourning or weeping.

# PSALM 18

*I call upon the LORD. . .so I shall be saved*
*from my enemies.*

◈

Psalm 18 is really two psalms merged into one. Its title—a psalm of David, the servant of the Lord—was devised much later than the psalm itself. The title was taken from 2 Samuel 22, where David recites this psalm and thus it was erroneously attributed to him as the author. Let us see it as two psalms, one composed of verses 1 to 30, the other of verses 31 to 50.

Verses 1 to 30 are clearly a celebration and thanksgiving to God for a victory of national import over an opposing army. Is it David's victory over Saul's army? How is it to become our personal prayer? Wherever there is a national or international triumph over unjust aggression of enemy forces, the hand of God is to be seen. We can praise and thank him for it in the past, present, and even future events! It should be for us a prayer of hope for ourselves or for any downtrodden people.

The power and protection of God is likened to a rock, a fortress, a shield, and a stronghold. It is a reminder that we can turn to him whenever we are threatened by the snares of death. Our cry will reach his ears, and no matter what powers are attacking us—even the power of death—God will deliver us into resurrection with his Christ.

In the midst of these cataclysmic forces, God reaches down from heaven, delivers me from the powers arrayed against me, and sets me down in a peaceful, open space. He does this because he delights in me. This is why verse 19 contains those beautiful words "because [the LORD] delighted in me." He is pleased when I remind him of that love and responds to it.

17

When I try to live the Christ-life that I have been given, I can claim *his* innocence, *his* purity, and *his* loyalty. My darkness fades in the brightness of the Lord's light, and I can do anything in him who gives me strength. His way is perfect and his promises are true.

Verses 31 to 50 are a statement of such decisive victory over enemies that it may be difficult for a man or woman who is a pacifist to pray it. If this is the case, then perhaps it should simply be omitted. However, it can also be interpreted on another level. Enemies can refer to those powers deep within our own false selves wherein hide our shadow sides. Our pride, self-love, greed, and hatred are enemies. We depend on God's strength to enable us to overcome them; we count on his light to dissipate their darkness. We do not wish to be people of violence but to be delivered from them. We ask God to show us his steadfast love.

# PSALM 19

*Let the words of my mouth and the meditation of
my heart be acceptable to you, O LORD, my rock
and my redeemer.*

∽

The last verse of this psalm could well be put first as a meditation and a prayer: "Let the words of my mouth and the meditation of my heart be acceptable to you, O LORD." In the first half of Psalm 19, we join our voices with the silent, constant praise of God's creation. The heavens tell his glory and proclaim his handiwork. There is no speech, nor are there words, yet the voice of creation goes out to all the earth. The sun rises and runs its course through the heavens and nothing escapes its light.

Just as God's work in the firmament declares his glory, so does his law revive the soul, make wise the simple, and gladden the heart. As in all the wisdom psalms, the Torah is described in many ways. It is the Law of the Lord, his testimony, his precepts, and his commands. God is the Creator of nature and the Giver of the Law.

As the brilliance of the sun casts light throughout the world, so do the ordinances of the Lord shine forth in our souls to expose even our hidden faults and purify us from errors that we are not even aware of. Then we can be truly blameless and innocent.

# PSALM 20

*Our pride is in the name of the LORD our God.*

This psalm constitutes a powerful and exuberant blessing given to the king before he sets forth with his army. He is standing at the gates of the Temple and has brought a lamb for sacrifice. The priests and the Levites stand before him and utter the words of this blessing: "May the LORD grant you your heart's desire." He is called the anointed of the Lord. In Hebrew this means the messiah. Confidence in God is expressed as being more certain than the power of chariots and horses.

For us as we pray this psalm, the anointed of the Lord is, first of all, Christ. Then we too—as members of his kingdom and sharers in his royal priesthood—are anointed. This happens at our baptism and again at our confirmation. So this psalm can be prayed as our acclamation at the victory of Christ in establishing his kingdom and for ourselves that we shall rise and stand upright in the face of our enemies.

# PSALM 21

*You bestow on him blessings forever; you make him glad with the joy of your presence.*

∽

No doubt this psalm is connected with the previous one. In Psalm 20, promises are made to the king in the form of blessings. Psalm 21 is a hymn of thanksgiving for these same blessings. It is sung or spoken by the Temple priest or prophet who adds, from verse 8 on, an oracle foretelling future accomplishments. It is very easy for us to pray along in verses 1 to 8 in gratitude to God for exalting his son, Jesus Christ, to his rightful place. When Jesus is exalted, we who have been invited to sit at his right hand in his kingdom also are glorified. Verse 8 and following can well be skipped over in accordance with Jesus' interpretation of the Great Commandment, "You have heard it said...but I say to you." He may even have had this psalm in mind when he warned us that we were called to pray for our enemies and do good to those who hate us.

# PSALM 22

*He did not hide his face from me, but heard when I cried to him.*

∽

St. Matthew tells us in chapter 15 of his Gospel that Jesus uttered this incredible prayer on the cross. Matthew gives us only the first line: "My God, my God, why have you forsaken me?" But we are to understand that Jesus prayed the entire psalm. We also understand that Psalm 22 is messianic and christological; that is, it is a direct reference to the passion and death of Jesus on the cross. Jesus begins almost in despair as he cries out to his Father who seems to have abandoned him. Yet, at the same time, he acknowledges that his Father is holy and dwells in the holy of holies in the Temple just a few hundred yards away from the site of the crucifixion. He is "enthroned on the praises of Israel" because the city is filled with Jews from all over the world, gathering before the Temple for the feast of Passover.

Jesus reminds his Father that in the past his ancestors trusted him and he delivered them. Jesus, however, is allowed to suffer indignities beyond conception. He is "a worm, and not human." He is mocked by bystanders who have come here just for this purpose. "Commit your cause to the LORD; let him deliver—let him rescue the one in whom he delights." In great sorrow, Jesus reminds his Father that he had protected him from his very birth. He had received him from his mother's womb. This was the role of a father, to receive the child as soon as it was born, thus acknowledging before all that it is his son. Jesus now pleads with his Father, "Do not be far from me....There is no one to help."

Jesus opens his eyes on the cross and sees only his persecutors. They are like wild bulls and roaring lions, while he is so weak and disjointed that he is poured out like water and his heart is melted like wax. He cries out, "I thirst." His strength is dried up like a potsherd and his tongue sticks to his jaws. He lies in the very dust of death. He cries out to his Father, "My hands and feet have shriveled; I can count all my bones. They stare and gloat over me; they divide my clothing among themselves."

At this point, an astounding change takes place. This is not unusual to see in a psalm of lamentation. Jesus is no longer in despair, but is able to plead with his Father to hasten to his aid and to deliver his soul. He becomes so confident of his rescue that he promises his Father that he will stand in the congregation—by this he means in his own synagogue in Nazareth, as was the custom—and proclaim to them everything that God has done for him. They will rejoice with him and glorify God who has heard when he cried to him. But Jesus does not stop here. He then promises to offer his praise in the *great* congregation. This means the Temple in Jerusalem. He even vows a sacrifice, traditionally a lamb or a kid goat, that will be used to feed the poor who will then praise the Lord in gratitude. But we know that he refers to himself as the Lamb of God who will feed his faithful with his Eucharistic body and blood.

Keep in mind that Jesus is still on the cross and suffering as he offers this prayer. He is so confident of his Father's gracious mercy that he cannot stop proclaiming how he will tell all the world of his Father's goodness. "All the ends of the earth shall remember and turn to the LORD." He will even go to the Gentiles, the families of the nations, because God rules over them also. One would think that he would have to stop at this point but Jesus goes even further. Now he proclaims that he will go to the dead, to all who go down to the dust. In his incredible hope and exuberance, Jesus must go even further in proclaiming his gratitude and joy in the mercy of his heavenly Father. Even while he suffers on the cross, Jesus expresses the joy of his deliverance. He will now go to the only place left where he has not yet proclaimed the glory of God. He will go to the future! "Posterity will serve him; future generations will be told about the Lord, and proclaim his deliverance to a people yet unborn, saying that he has done it." It is at this point that Jesus bows his head and hands over his spirit, not in defeat, but in a triumphant victory over death.

We should never forget that this incredible prayer is given to us to make it our own.

# PSALM 23

*I shall dwell in the house of the LORD
my whole life long.*

✺

This hymn of praise is undoubtedly one of the most beautiful and popular in the Psalter. Jesus certainly knew this psalm and was pleased to identify himself as the Good Shepherd. Not only does he provide materially for his sheep, leading them to green pastures and still waters, but also he restores their souls and leads them in the paths of righteousness. Verse 4 can be said to hearken back to Psalm 22 when Jesus literally was walking through the valley of the shadow of death. God is seen as a gracious host providing hospitality, anointing his guests with oil, and filling their cups to overflowing.

We are indeed the anointed of God. We are invited to his banquet. We are given his cup to drink, the cup of everlasting salvation. Goodness and mercy are personified as though they were two people who consistently follow us along the paths of righteousness. What a joy it is to state with such confidence that we shall dwell in the house of the Lord forever.

# PSALM 24

*Who shall ascend the hill of the Lord? And who shall
stand in his holy place?*

✺

Because God has created the earth, founded it upon seas, and established upon the rivers, he is the Creator and the fullness of the earth belongs to him. We must ask ourselves here, what we have done to the fullness of the earth. Certainly God has created it, but he has given it to us to care for it.

This is a liturgical psalm and it has to do with the return of the ark of the covenant to its rightful place in the Temple after it had been carried in battle. The priests are approaching the Temple gates bearing the ark upon their shoulders. Those standing within the gates are announcing the expectations placed upon those who carried the ark; that is, only those with clean hands and pure hearts. The ark is considered to be so great that the gates of the Temple must grow larger in order to receive it. "Lift up your heads, O gates, that the King of glory may come in." The chorus then chants the question, "Who is this King of glory?" And the priests carrying the ark respond, "The LORD of hosts, he is the King of glory!" It is important for us to be aware that the King of glory now dwells in temples made not of stone but of the hearts of all the faithful.

# PSALM 25

*Lead me in your truth, and teach me, for you are the God of my salvation.*

∽

This psalm begins with a bold statement, "To you, O LORD, I lift up my soul." We know, however, that it is not as simple as that. We are told that no one can even say, "Jesus is Lord," unless he be given the power by the Holy Spirit. But the very fact that the words of this psalm are given to us by the Lord gives us confidence that it is the Lord who lifts up our souls by his grace and because of his love. Indeed, in him do we put our trust. Following the theme of the first psalm of the Psalter, we again pray that the Lord will lead us in his truth and guide us in his paths. The motivation for this is not that *we* are just but that the Lord is merciful. His goodness and his steadfast love can be relied upon. How confident we should be, as we realize in our daily life that the paths we follow are the Lord's. To fear the Lord, to be in awe of his love and his majesty and his generosity, is to be humble and to receive his instructions. Those who fear the Lord are his true friends and he will be gracious to them.

# PSALM 26

*O Lord, I love the house in which you dwell,*
*and the place where your glory abides.*

✑

The opening words of this psalm could be spoken only by Christ: "Vindicate me, O LORD, for I have walked in my integrity." Yet because of our baptism, we as Christians are given a union with Christ so that he can speak these words on our behalf. It is a very bold thing to say the words of the second verse, "Prove me, O LORD, and try me." Someone has said that we should be very careful for what we pray lest we receive it. However, the next verse reassures us, because his steadfast love is ever before our eyes. Once again the theme of the first psalm in the Psalter is brought to mind: not sitting with false men but walking in faithfulness.

This psalm is a liturgical one used in the Temple while the psalmist undergoes some kind of ritual purification. We still use verse 6 in a liturgical context at the Eucharist when the priest says, as he washes his hands after the offering, "I wash my hands in innocence, and go about your altar, O LORD." He sings a song of thanksgiving: no doubt, this very psalm. And he then tells all his friends who have accompanied him of the favors that God has blessed him with. Just as Jesus proclaims in Psalm 22, the psalmist cries out, "In the great congregation I will bless the LORD." It is very easy to make this psalm our own and we should pray it periodically to maintain our sense of joy and gratitude.

# PSALM 27

*The LORD is the stronghold of my life;*
*of whom shall I be afraid?*

∽

This is a hymn of joy, gratitude, and thanksgiving. How easy it is to pray and to identify with the divinely inspired sentiments it expresses. Just the first line lifts up the heart in confidence and hope: "The LORD is my light and my salvation." There is no room in my life for fear. There is no need for me to look elsewhere for wisdom and guidance on my spiritual journey. Yes, I will experience difficulties. I will be attacked by enemies from within and without, but I will be safe, dwelling within the house of God and beholding his beauty. I will praise God in his temple and he will respond with that incredible command, "Seek my face." This gives me the courage that I need to pursue my spiritual journey. The Lord will teach and guide me and I will experience his goodness, even in this life. I will wait for the Lord because he gives me hope. I hear him speak to me in the voice of his Christ: "Come! Follow me."

# PSALM 28

*The LORD is my strength and my shield;*
*in him my heart trusts.*

༄

At the time this psalm was written, death was seen as the entrance into a shadowy, vague underworld where there was no communication with God. It was spoken of as "going down to the pit." The psalmist is standing before the entrance of the sanctuary raising his arms in the customary gesture of prayer and pleading with God to hear his cry. He is a living member of God's people and not a dead man; nor is he a worker of evil, a liar, or a hypocrite.

In reading this psalm, one cannot help thinking of the story of the publican and the Pharisee told by Jesus. It does sound like the psalmist is taking the role of the Pharisee—proclaiming his innocence while denouncing the sins of his neighbor. It is only if we pray this psalm in the name of Jesus, taking upon ourselves his innocence, that it will not be pharisaical or hypocritical.

The psalmist knows that God will hear his prayer, and so he thanks him for already doing so. If we are praying together with Jesus, we can say his words with great confidence: "The LORD is my strength and my shield." We are not alone, and if God answers our prayers—he answers the prayers of all his people. "Be their shepherd, and carry them forever."

# PSALM 29

*The voice of the LORD is over the waters;*
*the God of glory thunders.*

∽

It might surprise some people to learn that this psalm is actually from an ancient song to the pagan god Baal. In fact, it is only one of many passages found in the inspired Scriptures, taken from pagan sources. The Jewish writer sanctifies them, if you will, because of their appropriateness. Jumping ahead at least 3,000 years, we see the Church of the Second Vatican Council approving of such procedures when it tells us to dialogue with other religions and to learn from them.

It is a magnificent psalm, extolling God and seeing his glory and power manifesting itself in a storm. Anyone who has spent a summer in the Holy Land knows the awesome, sudden, and even frightening appearance of a thunderstorm. "The God of glory thunders....The LORD breaks the cedars of Lebanon...and flashes forth flames of fire...and strips the forest bare." The people gathered in the Temple, which symbolizes for them the heavens where God is seated on his throne, and then cry out and join their voices to the roaring thunder: "The LORD sits enthroned as king forever. May the LORD give strength to his people." It can today be a thrilling experience to stand outside in the weather praying this psalm as a thunderstorm approaches. The God of nature himself provides the setting for this liturgy.

# PSALM 30

*O LORD my God, I cried to you for help,*
*and you have healed me.*

⁓

As with so many of the other psalms, we can easily identify with this hymn of thanksgiving. At the moment, the psalmist is grateful for a healing he has experienced. Notice that he considers his illness "the enemy." He is very much aware that there are moments in his life when he does not experience gratitude. "Weeping may linger for the night, but joy comes with the morning." Life is full of ups and downs, joy and sorrow, suffering and consolations. They all come from the hand of God, "but his anger is only for a moment, and his favor is for a lifetime." So even with the ups and downs of good and bad times, we should praise the Lord. He turns my mourning into dancing and girds me with gladness, that my soul may praise him forever. The decisive and abiding model for this psalm is Jesus crucified. It was a time of sadness, suffering, and almost despair, yet it was but a moment. The resurrection is forever!

# PSALM 31

*Let your face shine upon your servant;*
*save me in your steadfast love.*

⁓

This is a typical psalm of lamentation, the most common type of psalm in the Psalter. In fact, it is really two psalms that parallel each other. The first is found in verses 1 to 8. It follows the classic structure for a lamentation. We have a cry for help, then a description of the psalmist's affliction, an expression of confidence in God, a protestation of innocence, followed by grateful recognition for God's help. This pattern is also followed in the second part, verses 9 to 24. We should see "the enemies" as all of the afflictions that we endure in our daily lives—personal and social, individual and collective. This involves not only personal illnesses, relationship crises, financial burdens, and psychological difficulties, but also worldwide issues such as famine and poverty, war and violence, injustice and persecution. These issues cause us to turn to the Lord and acknowledge his abundant goodness and his steadfast love. They cause us to call upon the whole Church, and pray, "Love the LORD, all you his saints!" We end with a prayer of hope and confidence, "Be strong, and let your heart take courage, all you who wait for the LORD!"

# PSALM 32

*Be glad in the LORD and rejoice, O righteous,*
*and shout for joy, all you upright in heart.*

∞

At three places within this psalm of thanksgiving, there is a curious liturgical rubric. The word, placed beside the verses of the psalm, is *Selah*. This indicates a point for a pause or at least a musical interlude in the psalm for purposes of meditation. Clearly the purpose is to give emphasis to a particular verse. The first pause causes us to reflect upon our weakness, in particular our physical weakness. What physical weaknesses do we have and what is their relationship to sin? The psalmist believed there was a direct connection. Now, because his physical ailment is healed, he feels assured that God has forgiven his sins, which he acknowledges in the presence of the congregation. We who are under the headship of Christ, do not see a necessary connection between our illnesses and our personal sins. Just as Christ, who is sinless, suffered on the cross, so too do we suffer that we might make up in our own bodies what is lacking in the sufferings of Christ. We are called to share in Christ's redemption of the world through our sufferings; that is, through our own personal crosses.

The second *Selah* causes us to pause after, "You forgave the guilt of my sin." The emphasis here is not on the sin but rather on the forgiveness. Perhaps here we should pause to reflect on the many times God has forgiven us for our sins of thought, word, deed, and omission. We may have sinned greatly, but this simply proves that God's love is even greater.

The third *Selah* is found after this beautiful verse: "You are a hiding place for me; you preserve me from trouble; you surround me with glad cries of deliverance." What a consolation it is to be able to pray these words that refer now, not so much to the past, but to God's continued forgiveness and protection in the future. How appropriate it is that we conclude this psalm with rejoicing and a shout for joy!

# PSALM 33

*Praise the LORD with the lyre; make melody to him*
*with the harp of ten strings.*

∽

This beautiful psalm was no doubt originally written to be performed with liturgical splendor in the Temple. It was sung to the accompaniment of the lyre and harp, and with many voices. It harkens back to the creation stories in the Book of Genesis in extolling the might and power of the Lord's word. Because the Lord loves righteousness, he has filled the earth with his steadfast love. All the efforts of men and women, the might of armies, and the power of horses cannot bring about salvation. The word of the Lord is more powerful. God sees us who hope in his steadfast love.

The first three verses tell us how to make a joyful noise to the Lord. Praise him with the lyre, make melody with the harp, and with loud shouts sing him a new song. Every time we pray this psalm, it does become a new song because we add to it the originality of our personal faith and love. The word of the Lord, the breath of his mouth, speaks and the earth is full of his steadfast love. His word is the expression of the thoughts of his heart. The most beautiful thought of his heart, his very Word, is the Christ. He is the Word through whom all things were made and through whom, in the power of his Holy Spirit, creation continues inexorably toward the perfect end he has decreed for it. His Word expresses the thoughts of his heart and makes our hearts glad. We can get in touch with this gladness every time we pray this beautiful psalm.

# PSALM 34

*Come, O children, listen to me; I will teach you
the fear of the LORD.*

This hymn of thanksgiving is styled in the manner of the teachers of wisdom. It is an acrostic psalm; that is, in the original Hebrew, each verse begins with a different letter of the alphabet.

As we said earlier, by using different letters of the alphabet for each line, the psalm is understood to express everything that words can say. Perhaps this can be summed up in these words, "Oh taste and see that the LORD is good."

The psalm is replete with the advice, admonitions, and reflections so often found in wisdom literature. It is the fruit of the human experience as reflected on by wise men and women and now handed down to the young. Fidelity in uprightness and justice, hope inspired by God's steadfast love, and the subsequent joy resulting from this have all been experienced by the psalmist. He now uses this public celebration to express that joy and his gratitude. This psalm enables us to join with him with wisdom and with ease. The psalmist calls us to join him in exalting the name of the Lord. "Be radiant," he sings. The wise man and woman know that even the righteous will have their share of afflictions but the Lord will deliver them.

# PSALM 35

*Great is the LORD, who delights in*
*the welfare of his servant.*

∽

This is a lamentation psalm. There are three distinct units of lament; starting with verse I, verse I I, and verse I7. It is not the kind of psalm that a Christian would pray. Many of the lamentations could have been uttered by Christ. He certainly could have pleaded for God's support and ultimate deliverance. He could identify with the unjust and even malicious treatment he was given by his enemies. He could wonder why such treatment should come from people he had befriended and even accepted with familial love. He could not, however, wish on them the vengeance depicted in this psalm. "Vindicate me, O LORD, my God": for Jesus, this plea would actually mean, "Father, forgive them." This would be the way in which Jesus is vindicated. This would be the way in which his teachings would be demonstrated, not by wishing evil upon his enemies. This psalm does demonstrate, once again, the necessity of Jesus' new teaching in the Sermon on the Mount. When Jesus said, "You have heard it said," he was referring precisely to such Old Testament texts as Psalm 35. As a form of prayer, this would be best omitted from a Christian prayer book. Yet, there are some who would say that we might need such a prayer in the initial emotional throes of some particular suffering. We might need, at least temporarily, to express the vehemence of our pain, our anger, and our lack of understanding.

# PSALM 36

*Your steadfast love, O LORD, extends to the heavens,*
*your faithfulness to the clouds.*

There is a marked contrast in this psalm between verses 1 to 4 and verses 5 to 12. In the first part we have a description of how evil works upon a person; what it does, both internally and externally. We should apply this to ourselves. It is what happens to us when we stray from the law of the Lord. In contrast we see how the steadfast love of God works upon a person. Three times is this emphasized. It extends to the heavens, it is precious, and it is God's salvation to the upright of heart. Evil leads to further evil. Good leads to good. This is beautifully expressed in the line, "In your light we see light." Indeed, God's steadfast love is our light, and what we see from him and receive from him, we carry within ourselves and communicate to others. Jesus is the light of the world and we are called, not only to live in his light, but also to bring it to those who live in darkness.

# PSALM 37

*Be still before the LORD, and wait patiently for him.*

༄

This psalm is a beautiful extension of the theme from Psalm 1. It contrasts the way of the wicked and the way of the just. There is no need for us to lament and cry to the Lord to deliver us from the hands of evildoers. It is in the very nature of evil that it results in evil. It does not come from God and ultimately it cannot flourish. There is no need to fret. Simply trust in the Lord and he will vindicate you. He laughs at the wicked who inevitably fall into their own pits. The just may occasionally stumble but the Lord will support them.

As a wisdom psalm, this hymn is supposed to be the advice of an experienced older person. But is it altogether wise and verifiable through experience? He says, "I have been young, and now am old; yet I have not seen the righteous forsaken or their children begging bread." Most of us, as we look around in our societies, in our inner cities, and in many impoverished parts of the world, see the righteous forsaken and their children begging bread. It is simply not realistic to say otherwise. Yet it is the intent of the psalmist to express his unfaltering hope in his ultimate justification by God, "Wait for the LORD, and keep to his way." We all know of people who have demonstrated this hope—people who have suffered socially, economically, physically, and emotionally, and yet who have declared their trust in God. They are a source of comfort and edification for all who see them, and we know that ultimately God will be their vindicator.

# PSALM 38

*O LORD, all my longing is known to you;*
*my sighing is not hidden from you.*

⸙

This lamentation can be placed on the tongue of Jesus on the cross. And so it can also be placed on the tongues of all those members of his Body who are suffering today throughout the world. And it can be placed upon our tongues as we pray it in their name. The description of the psalmist's suffering is poignant and real, and it gets worse and worse in each subsequent verse, until he can describe himself only as a dead man. But even then he has hope: "But it is for you, O LORD, that I wait."

The sufferings of the psalmist are overwhelming. There is no soundness in his flesh or health in his bones. He is utterly crushed and his heart fails. This psalm expresses the voice of the suffering Christ on his cross and in his Body, the Church. Our hope is in God's steadfast love and on him do we wait. Our suffering is the very cause of our hope. It enables us to unite with the sufferings of Christ and with the entire human race. It summons forth from us, on behalf of the whole world, a cry of hope that touches the heart of God: "O my God, do not be far from me." Embracing this psalm, let us accept as our own all of the pain and misery afflicting the world this day even as Christ accepts it—with hope and love.

# PSALM 39

*Hear my prayer, O LORD, and give ear to my cry.*

∽

This is a starkly realistic psalm. and one we would do well to pray on a regular basis. The theme is found in verse 4: "LORD, let me know my end, and what is the measure of my days." Obviously the psalmist is very ill. He has not openly complained because he does not wish unbelievers to attribute his illness to God's lack of concern. Yet his distress grows worse until he reaches the point where he can no longer be silent. He begs the Lord for peace before he departs and is no more.

Our Christian faith gives us a greater hope than this poor man had. We believe that our departure in death will result in entering the fullness of God's kingdom. Indeed, we should keep the reality of our death always before our eyes. For what does it profit us if we should gain the whole world but suffer the loss of our souls?

# PSALM 40

*I delight to do your will, O my God;*
*your law is within my heart.*

∽

We have all experienced the mercy of God. He has preserved us from evils, strengthened us in our weakness, and given us hope. Notice how concretely the psalmist expresses these blessings. God has drawn him up from the desolate pit, out of the miry bog, set his feet upon a rock, and made his steps secure. And now, because God has inspired this psalm in his holy Scriptures, we can express literally the words of verse 3: "He put a new song in my mouth, a song of praise to our God."

In chapter 10 of the Letter to the Hebrews we have been given a christological interpretation of verses 6 to 9. "Sacrifice and offering you do not desire....I delight to do your will, O my God." These words are put into the mouth of Christ, and so they should also be put into our mouths. We fulfill God's will not in empty, external gestures, nor in idle words, but only when his law is within our hearts in sincerity and truth.

This psalm was probably originally two psalms. Verses 1 to 11 was a psalm of thanksgiving, and verses 12 to 17 was a psalm of lament.

# PSALM 41

*Blessed be the LORD, the God of Israel,*
*from everlasting to everlasting. Amen and Amen.*

෴

This psalm marks the end of the first book of the Psalter. This is indicated by verse 13, a doxology or praise of God that does not really belong to Psalm 41 but indicates the conclusion of the first book. The Psalter is divided somewhat artificially into five books, no doubt in imitation of the five books of the Torah.

Blessed is the Lord because he listens to the poor. The psalmist is referring to himself as the poor. We are to understand the meaning of the word *poor* in much the same way that we use it in our daily speech. We use it to refer, not only to those without money, but also to people of any financial status who are under-going difficulties that arouse our sympathy. The cries of such people will be heard by the Lord. Even though he is undergoing great distress, the psalmist knows that God is pleased with him because he has not been defeated. God is upholding him and will continue to do so for ever.

# BOOK TWO

# PSALMS
# 42 TO 72

# PSALM 42

*My soul thirsts for God, for the living God. When*
*shall I come and behold the face of God?*

∽

Psalm 42 and Psalm 43 are actually one psalm. They were probably separated for liturgical purposes, and so we have them in the
Psalter today as two prayers. Utilizing the ancient rabbinical
principle that nothing in the inspired word of God is without
special significance, we will look at each of them as having its
own messages.

Psalm 42's dramatic and poignant expression of longing for
God in his holy Temple in Jerusalem is reproducible today by the
faithful soul open to the workings of the Holy Spirit on a personal
level. This longing is even physical. The author evidently lives far
north of Jerusalem near Mount Hermon and the sources of the
Jordan River. He has seen the hart dipping its nose into the running waters to quench its thirst while he experiences, day and night,
only the moisture of his tears. He hears the roaring of the waters
of the Jordan. They do not satisfy his thirst but instead inundate
him with their power. He hears in them the voice of God calling
him with his steadfast love. He is sick with a deadly wound and
cannot make the required visit to the Temple. He takes himself to
task for being cast down, for he knows in his heart of hearts that
he will yet live to praise God as he desires.

To offer this hope-filled prayer with the psalmist is to experience his longing for God in our own lives. God is our rock and
his steadfast love is with us. Our very weaknesses call us to hope in
him, our savior and our God! Once again we are reminded of the
faith and hope of St. Paul: "When I am weak then I am strong."

# PSALM 43

*I will go to the altar of God,*
*to God my exceeding joy.*

∽

For centuries, the Church has used Psalm 43 at the beginning of the eucharistic liturgy. The longing for God, which is placed in the human heart by God himself, is universal. The psalmist seems to have been too ill to go from his dwelling place in the north of Israel, near Mount Hermon and the source of the Jordan River, to Jerusalem for one of the three required yearly pilgrimages. The longing or attraction for God is powerful and graphic—indeed almost physical, like a wild desert animal longing for running waters.

Very often when referring to God, Hebrew writers will use a circumlocution. Instead of referring directly to God, they will refer to his name. For example, they will say, "Blessed be his holy name" instead of "Blessed be God." Some claimed that no one could see the face of God and live, but in spite of this the psalmist boldly proclaims, "When shall I come [to Jerusalem] and behold the face of God?" He alternates between his sadness—brought about by his illness, his inability to make his pilgrimage, and the criticism of unbelievers—and his joy in the hope that he will yet be able to "again praise him, my help and my God." The Church has prayed this psalm for centuries to express her longing to come into the presence of God and to see his face, as it were, in his eucharistic presence.

# PSALM 44

*Rise up, come to our help. Redeem us for
the sake of your steadfast love.*

∽

In the Old Testament, when reference is made to the God of
Abraham, Isaac, or Jacob, the writer intends us to understand that
God is a personal God. God is not some abstract, transcendent,
indifferent creator but is the very God who made a covenant with
Abraham and his children; who watches over them, who visits
them, who chides and loves them like a father or mother. Psalm 44,
then, begins with a statement of the tradition of a personal God.
Everything that our ancestors received was given to them by a God
who loved them even enough to punish them for their own bene-
fit. This God of Jacob is the very God that we honor as our king.
It is only through him that we overcome our foes, internal and
external. In God alone can we make our boast.

In spite of the fact that God permits us to suffer and that
hostile forces often get the better of us, our hearts have not been
turned away nor have our footsteps deviated from the paths of justice. So God permits us to remind him (really, to remind ourselves)
of the things he has done for us in the past, both for our fathers
and for ourselves. Thus we are encouraged to urge him, "Rise up,
come to our help!" This prayer should be on our lips daily, even
many times a day.

# PSALM 45

*Grace is poured upon your lips;*
*therefore God has blessed you forever.*

This is a song written by a court musician for the wedding of the king. We can interpret it christologically as being about Christ and his love for the Church, and for the individual soul. We may not have the talents of that musician, but we can sing his song as the Lord gives it to us in this psalm.

We praise the Christ ("God has anointed you") and acknowledge his splendor, as he stands at the right hand of the Father in glory. We also acknowledge his queen, who stands by his side clothed in golden splendor. This is the Church; indeed, it is we ourselves, as members of that Church. The very angels accompany us with joy and gladness into the house of God, and our names will be celebrated forever. This is not just an elaborate illusion, but simply a poetic expression of the joys that God has promised to those who love him.

# PSALM 46

*The LORD of hosts is with us;*
*the God of Jacob is our refuge.*

Because of its emphasis on Jerusalem as the Holy City, this psalm, like some others, is called a Song of Zion. Today, among certain Christians, there is a great emphasis on the last days and the final judgment. This is often seen as a time of cataclysmic horror and physical, terrestrial upheavals. This poem, however, is one of triumphant joy, security, and confidence in the power of God as our refuge.

To the degree that this horror and these upheavals are present, we need not fear because God is our refuge and our strength. The Jerusalem spoken of here is the New Jerusalem, which the Book of Revelation speaks of as descending from heaven like a bride adorned for her wedding.

The New Jerusalem is the Church, and the final gathering of the people of God. In fact, there is no river anywhere near Jerusalem, but ideally or mythically, God's city would be made perfect by the presence of an abundant flowing of water. In the last days, nations will rage and kingdoms will totter, but God will be in control. His voice will be heard above the tumult: "Be still, and know that I am God!" He is the Lord of hosts; that is, the Lord of armies. His armies, as Jesus tells us, are made up of angels, and they are with us. This psalm was the inspiration behind Martin Luther's magnificent song, "A Mighty Fortress Is Our God." The image of God as Lord of hosts, a military leader, may not be pleasing to many Christians. However, let us remember that this Lord makes wars cease to the end of the earth.

"Be still, and know that I am God" is often quoted in reference to contemplative meditation, a meditation in which one is placed in awesome silence before God. Obviously, this is not the meaning of the verse within the context of this psalm. However, it can be used for the purpose of meditation in what we call an "accommodated sense."

# PSALM 47

*God is king over the nations;
God sits on his holy throne.*

☙

This triumphant hymn is an invitation to those gathered before
the Temple to praise God as the ark of the covenant is returned
to the holy of holies after leading the people in victorious battle.
As the Temple is a symbol of the cosmos, the singing and clap-
ping of the people is to extend throughout the world because
God is a great king over all the earth.

When the ark is returned to its place, the belief was that God
sat enthroned on the mercy seat above it. All the rulers of the
nations are called to gather here in praise. We can pray this psalm
as an expression of our hope and our faith in the ultimate triumph
of God's kingdom.

# PSALM 48

*Great is the LORD.....His holy mountain, beautiful
in elevation, is the joy of all the earth.*

☙

This is another Song of Zion, an idealistic, mythical description
of the New Jerusalem, the city established by our God to last forever. This, indeed, is the Church as the fulfillment of God's kingdom. The greatest tribute we can give to God in the midst of his
Church is to contemplate his steadfast love. This is the way that we
will tell the coming generations that God is our God forever.

God's holy mountain, Mount Zion in Jerusalem, is the joy of all the earth. There is an easy transition here from the city of the great king to the mythical city in Revelation:

> And I saw the holy city, the new Jerusalem, coming down out of heaven from God, prepared as a bride adorned for her husband. And I heard a great voice from the throne saying,
>
> "See, the home of God is among mortals.
> He will dwell with them;
> they will be his peoples
> and God himself will be with them;
> he will wipe away every tear from their eyes.
> Death will be no more;
> mourning and crying and pain will be no more,
> for the first things have passed away." (Rev 21:2–4)

The psalm concludes with a call for a procession about the city walls: "Walk about Zion, go all around it, count its towers." The future is filled with hope because God will guide his Church. Pray this psalm for and together with the Church. This is our future!

# PSALM 49

*God will ransom my soul from the power of Sheol,*
*for he will receive me.*

～

This is a wonderful example of a wisdom psalm. It is a meditation on the transience of life and material possessions. One can imagine it coming from the lips of a wise old man, a teacher of youth, as he shares the experiences of his long life. Jesus is the quintessential wise man. He did not fear in times of trouble, and he called us to place our faith and confidence in the Father. He taught us what true wealth is and urged us to store up for ourselves treasures in heaven. There is great profit in praying this psalm, given to us by the Holy Spirit, to remind us of all the truths that Jesus taught.

# PSALM 50

*Offer to God a sacrifice of thanksgiving,*
*and pay your vows to the Most High.*
*Call on me in the day of trouble;*
*I will deliver you and you shall glorify me.*

❧

This is an awesome meditation on the judgment of God. His judgment is meted out to all the nations on the earth and to his people, good and evil. He is not appeased by empty, liturgical ceremonies. What does the sacrifice of animals mean to him? He owns them all anyhow. If he were hungry, would he tell us? The only thing that we can give him is our personal thanksgiving and fidelity in honoring our commitments to him. We must not speak deceit, nor slander our brothers, nor accompany evildoers. We must worship God, as Jesus commands, in spirit and in truth.

# PSALM 51

*Create in me a clean heart, O God,*
*and put a new and right spirit within me.*

∽

This psalm is one of the seven traditional penitential psalms for Christians. For over 1,500 years, Christians have recited it at the beginning of Lauds (Morning Prayer). It differs from similar psalms of lamentation in that the psalmist does not protest his innocence or complain about persecution from his enemies. The sublimity of his thought is seen in the very first verse where he pleads for the mercy of God simply because of its abundance. This psalm is not only a plea for forgiveness, but a plea and a resolution for personal renewal: "Create in me a clean heart."

The Christian teaching on original sin is anticipated in this psalm. The psalmist inherits the general sinfulness of mankind but also contributes to it through his personal offenses. Mere ritual sacrifice is useless when it is not accompanied by genuine sorrow and the determination to reform. Instead of vowing a sacrifice, he promises to lead sinners back to God, in accordance with the elevated nature of this prayer, by his example and teaching. The last two verses are later additions, seeking to mollify the sensitivities of Temple priests and servants by asserting that, after they give to God their broken and contrite hearts, he will receive their offerings and sacrifices. This psalm was probably written in the sixth century BC, after the Babylonian exile but before the walls and the Temple of Jerusalem were restored. It is one that could well be recited by Christians daily.

# PSALM 52

*I will thank you forever,*
*because of what you have done.*

∽

When we pray this psalm, who is the "mighty one" of the first verse who plots destruction, speaks deceit, and loves evil more than good? This should not be seen as a diatribe against people whom we consider our enemies. Rather, it should be seen as a prayer in which we acknowledge that ultimately God will vindicate the just and that goodness will triumph over evil. We need to be assured of this from time to time, especially when the evils that man visits upon man confront us daily. We live in a moral universe over which God reigns. His kingdom is all around us, even though at times it may seem that the power of evil has conquered it. The theme of Psalm I is recalled here in verse 8: "But I am like a green olive tree in the house of God." And God himself puts into our mouths the beautiful words, "I trust in the steadfast love of God forever and ever."

# PSALM 53

*When God restores the fortunes of his people,*
*Jacob will rejoice; Israel will be glad.*

∽

Sometimes there is a real human need to vent our anxiety, our discouragement, and even our pessimistic, weak, human outlook on the status of things. Even though, inspired by faith, we know in our heart of hearts that it is not true, we feel that there is no one who does good and that we are surrounded by fools who say in their hearts, if not with their lips, that there is no God. Psalm 53 allows us to do this only because it will then carry us above such discouragement. Deliverance will come for us and we shall be glad and rejoice!

# PSALM 54

*Surely, God is my helper;*
*the Lord is the upholder of my life.*

∼

The title of this psalm is "A Maskil of David, when the Ziphites went and told Saul, 'David is hiding among us.'" Like all the psalm titles, it was added on by an editor centuries after the psalm itself was written. There was a tendency then to try to see a Davidic element in all the psalms. This one, however, was probably written centuries after the time of David. It is a typical, personal, lamentation psalm and follows the classic pattern: cry for help, complaint, thanksgiving, and vow.

Although it is quite brief, this psalm can be the source for deep reflection. In the usual tradition, the psalmist expresses outraged innocence. No doubt he really believes that this is the case. It is not difficult, however, to imagine his "enemies" praying the exact same psalm for themselves. How often have we had this situation in wars, and even civil strife, where both sides prayed to the same God with the same outraged innocence? The only safe response to this uncomfortable situation is to follow the admonition of Jesus and to pray for our enemies instead of cursing them.

The psalmist begins by invoking God's name and its power. He ends with giving thanks to his name for it is good. This whole

53

psalm can be seen as an example of St. Paul's teaching that we should find our strength in Christ and that, consequently, it is when we are weak that we are strong.

# PSALM 55

*I call upon God, and the LORD will save me.*

∞

This psalm was probably recited in the Temple where the priests, who played a role in its recitation, greeted the psalmist. Verse 22, "Cast your burden on the LORD, and he will sustain you," is probably an oracle uttered by the priests in response to the psalmist's cry for help.

It can be a heartbreaking experience to pray this psalm sincerely: the adversary is a familiar friend and companion with whom the psalmist used to hold sweet conversation within God's house, as they walked in friendship. Perhaps we have had such an experience. We know that Jesus did, when almost all of his friends abandoned him, especially Judas and Peter. Daily, all over the world, people are betrayed by friends, by companions who broke bread with them. Pray this psalm for yourself and for your brothers and sisters.

There are two speakers in this psalm, the psalmist himself, who gives the lamentation, and the Temple priests, who respond. You can see this in verse 9 possibly, but definitely in verse 15 and in the final verse 22, where the petitioner is given an assurance of God's protection. We should read this blessing as given to us.

# PSALM 56

*In God I trust; I am not afraid.*
*What can a mere mortal do to me?*

∞

Again, as in previous lamentation psalms, we should consider the "enemies" as afflictions of any kind that we are called to endure in this life. The real tragedy of this psalm is only partially found in the afflictions of its author, but can be seen in the fact that this psalm was given as a liturgical formula so that others could use it also. It is expressive of the unfortunate situation found in the community where betrayal was so common. When we consider the afflictions that confront our world today, are we so different? We definitely need to make these words our own: "When I am afraid I put my trust in you."

Putting one's tears in a bottle was a practice in the psalmist's day. We know that it was not unusual in some of the surrounding cultures. Putting them in his book is in accordance with the tradition that God's recording angel kept records of each individual. It is along the same idea expressed by Jesus when he said that not even a sparrow falls without his heavenly Father taking note of it. God sees our afflictions and he remembers them. This is why he can say, "In God I trust; I am not afraid. What can a mere mortal do against me?"

# PSALM 57

*Awake, my soul! Awake, O harp and lyre!*
*I will awake the dawn.*

As we have seen in other psalms, Psalm 57 is a composite of two distinct hymns: a lamentation and a thanksgiving. The first unit, verses 1 to 4 and verse 6, is an unoriginal lamentation that repeats the contents and the imagery of other laments. The second unit is quite original, imaginative, and poetic. Verses 7 to 11 have an entirely different tone from the previous verses. They seem to have a relationship to some of the verses in Psalm 108. It is easy and pleasant to join in with the psalmist's sentiments as he says, "My heart is steadfast, O my God, my heart is steadfast. I will sing and make melody. Awake, my soul! Awake, O harp and lyre! I will awake the dawn."

# PSALM 58

*Surely there is a God who judges on earth.*

The gods of verse 1 should be seen as those people in power whose duty it is to judge with justice. Not infrequently did Israel undergo periods of lawlessness and corruption, especially in the higher echelons. The psalmist sees himself as counterattacking this wickedness through the magic of his curses.

Such injustices are not unknown in our day. To see them being flagrantly practiced in all parts of the world may cause us to question the goodness of God. We can be angry with God. Sometimes anger even is a prayer. The magic, however, is seen in the power of Christian love and in the assurance that there is a God who judges on earth as in heaven.

# PSALM 59

*Protect me from those who rise up against me.*

∽

This psalm is a prime example of the kind of prayer that we do *not* want to make. Psalm 59 is especially bitter and vindictive and certainly could not be prayed by a Christian. However, it could be used as a meditation. There are such evils in the world and such evil people. We confront them daily in our newspapers and on our television sets. It is good for us, at least, to do this in terms of our relationship with God. Not that we wish to repay evil with evil, but that we wish to be reminded that God is on his throne above the heavens as well is in the midst of his people, and that we can trust in him. This psalm also reminds us that the fruits of evil are themselves evil. God permits evil that good may come from it, just as he permitted the crucifixion of his Son that the world might know of his love. But on a personal level, evildoers will fall into their own pits, if not in this life then before God in judgment. At the same time, such a meditation should prompt us to pray for evildoers. May they be receptive of God's love and of the fruits of that love. This is the way that our Lord prefers to do away with evildoers and why he changed the Law of the Talon ("An eye for an eye") to the Golden Rule ("Do unto others").

# PSALM 60

*Grant us help against the foe,*
*for human help is worthless.*

&infin;

Earlier, an oracle had been uttered in the Temple by which God promised that Israel would conquer her enemies in all the countries that surrounded her: Shechem, Gilead, Moab, Edom, and Philistia. But here, God has been angry and his people have suffered hard things. They have been given a bitter wine to drink.

Actually, the psalmist is calling for the restoration of all the nations that once made up the United Monarchy. We know that God is behind everything that happens and that he even sustains in being all that exists. Nothing happens outside of his will, and even when evil is perpetrated, God must permit it. In a war, does God choose sides? He does not seem always to prefer Israel over her enemies. Must we not say the same thing today? Does God choose our side? If he does not, why? What if those on the "other side" pray to him with equal sincerity and conviction? These are not easy questions to answer. Perhaps the chief value of this psalm is that it raises the questions. At any rate, we can make the final petition our own: "With God we shall do valiantly."

# PSALM 61

*Let me abide in your tent forever,*
*find refuge under the shelter of your wings.*

∽

This prayer is put into the mouth of the Temple priests who pray for their king, and so we can appropriately place it in the mouth of Jesus and in the mouths of all his followers who make up his kingdom. The Lord is our rock, our refuge, a strong tower, a sheltering tent; he is like an eagle protecting its young under the shelter of its wings. I will sing praises to God's name every day because of his steadfast love and faithfulness. We make our own the praises that have been sung to the Lord for over 2,500 years and that will continue to be sung until he comes in glory.

Originally, the psalmist did not live in Jerusalem but cried out to God from the ends of the earth. Now he is on pilgrimage and, like us, longs for the protection of God's house. He is assured of this because Christ, the King of Kings, sits at the Father's right hand enthroned in love and fidelity.

# PSALM 62

*For God alone my soul waits in silence,*
*for my hope is from him.*

∽

All of our sins are forms of idolatry in which we place our trust in something other than God. Indeed, it is worshiping false gods to prefer anything to the Lord our God. We cannot put our trust

59

in wealth, in human resources, or in men of high or low estate. Again and again, we affirm that God alone is our salvation, our fortress, our deliverance and our honor. He is our refuge and we trust in him at all times. Power belongs to God. His resources are unlimited, and he alone is to be the object of our steadfast love.

For God alone our souls wait in silence. This is what contemplative prayer is all about: waiting for the Lord in stillness, the silent awesome appreciation of God's power, and the return of his steadfast love. Twice the psalmist repeats that we wait in silence. In this way, we come to realize that God is our hope and our salvation. All else is nothing.

# PSALM 63

*O God...I seek you, my soul thirsts for you...*
*as in a dry and weary land where there is no water.*

⁓

Methodist bishop William W. Hutchinson has described this psalm as "one of the truly notable bits of devotional writing in all the literature of religion." It is ascribed to the king in verse 11, but this is probably a later addition. It is not a hymn about God but rather a prayer offered directly and personally to God. It anticipates the manner of the great mystics who expressed the depths of their union with God in the language of physical needs and satisfactions. "My soul thirsts for you; my flesh faints for you, as in a dry and weary land." Mystical union comes about through the splendor of the Temple liturgy in the consciousness of God's presence within it. Again the physical expression of total satisfaction in the reality of God and of his love is like a feast for the soul filled with marrow and fat. The mind reflects on the glory of God in the shadows of the night; the mouth praises him with joyful lips and the soul clings to him. What a joy to praise God in this psalm and to allow the Holy Spirit himself to articulate such an expression of our love and personal intimacy.

# PSALM 64

*Let the righteous rejoice in the LORD*
*and take refuge in him.*

૭૦

The only way to redeem this psalm is to interpret it allegorically, and there are great truths to be found that way. We can focus on two verses: verse 3, which complains about enemies who aim bitter words like arrows, and verse 7, which states that God will shoot his arrow at these enemies and they will be suddenly wounded. We must be aware that God has no enemies. He has only children whom he loves. Our heavenly Father is perfect and he makes his rain fall and his sun shine on the just and the unjust alike.

Some of the great mystics have expressed God's love as a wounding, caused by his arrow of love. While sinners can wound one another by bitter words like arrows, God's arrows can only strengthen, heal, and love. God loves us while we are yet in sin. If this were not so, we could never turn to him in repentance. The psalmist says, "Let the righteous rejoice in the LORD and take refuge in him." We must remember that all those whom God wounds with his arrows of love become the righteous. So if we pray this psalm in bitterness, we must allow a Christian interpretation to turn it into forgiveness.

# PSALM 65

*Happy are those whom you choose and
bring near to live in your courts.*

∽

A true understanding of the meaning of this glorious psalm comes about simply by praying it. It is obviously a hymn of thanksgiving for a bounteous harvest but is indeed more than that. It has a larger meaning than its material implications. The bounty that God has bestowed on the land is a sign of his goodness and mercy. Nor is it limited to his chosen people: it extends to the ends of the earth and the farthest seas.

The blessing of having an abundance of water is a very strong motif. God visits the earth by watering it. There is a river of God providing for the grain. It is softened with showers that bless its growth, and the pastures of the wilderness drip with joy. This is even a symbol of the heavenly kingdom where the Book of Revelation speaks of the river of the water of life bright as crystal, flowing from the throne of God. It is through the waters of baptism that we are incorporated into the Body of Christ.

# PSALM 66

*Make a joyful noise to God, all the earth;
sing the glory of his name; give to him glorious praise.*

∽

We have just been told in Psalm 65 that God makes the outgoing of the morning and the evening to shout for joy. The meadows clothed with flocks, and the valleys decked with grain, also shout and sing together for joy. This refrain is taken up again in Psalm 66 where all the earth is called to sing his glorious praise and to make a joyful noise to God. God is praised for everything, including his wonderful works in history. He is even blessed and praised because of the trials with which he has tested his people and from which he has delivered them.

The psalmist sings this song as he approaches the Temple with his sacrifice, and he calls on all of those around him who fear God to listen while he tells what God has done for him. The gift of this inspired psalm allows us even today to join this shout of joy and praise. We can indeed praise God for his wonderful works in history and for his past gifts to every individual, including the psalmist. We bring it up to date by praising him for his wonderful works in our lives and for the blessings and gifts that he has given to those around us. Truly, God listens and gives heed to the voice of our prayer.

# PSALM 67

*May God continue to bless us;*
*let all the ends of the earth revere him.*

∽

There is a beautiful passage in the sixth chapter of the Book of Numbers:

> The Lord said to Moses, saying, "Speak to Aaron and his sons, saying, Thus you shall bless the Israelites: You shall say to them,

The Lord bless you and keep you:
the Lord make his face to shine upon you, and be
    gracious to you:
the Lord lift up his countenance upon you, and give
    you peace.

"So shall they put my name upon the Israelites, and I will bless them." (Num 6:23–27)

This is how this brief but beautiful psalm of thanksgiving begins. It is an effulgent outpouring of praise and thanksgiving on the occasion of an abundant harvest. The earth has yielded its increase and God has blessed us. Most of us today are unaware of the harvests. If they are sparse in some places, they are abundant in others, and we scarcely know where our food comes from. Some of us have never known a scarcity of food and for this, we should be grateful. The psalmist embraces the whole earth in his song of gratitude, and so should we as we acknowledge gratefully that our tables are filled with the produce of many nations, that our daily lives are supported and comforted by products from all over the world.

# PSALM 68

*Sing to God, O kingdoms of the earth;*
*sing praises to the Lord.*

This entire psalm is bound together by its last three words: "Blessed be God!" Everything in it acknowledges God's goodness, power, and righteousness. Most scholars think that this psalm is a collection of unrelated fragments. Yet to approach it as a prayer rather than analyze it as a poem gives one an experience of its purpose, which is to praise God for his wonderful works, for his justice in the world, for his mighty manifestations in nature, for his goodness to Israel. The description of the Temple procession, involving as it does the tribes and the Temple ministers, is to be seen as a microcosmic sacrament of the greater reality of God's glory, manifested in all the kingdoms of the earth and in the heavens. We should include our own lives in this listing of God's benevolent deeds.

# PSALM 69

*Do not hide your face from your servant,*
*for I am in distress—make haste to answer me.*

∽

When we pray this psalm, we sum up the pain, the aspirations, the hopes, the questions and, indeed, the blessings of the whole world. We can pray it in our own name and see its application in our own lives. We can pray it in the name of others and touch their sufferings, even their anger and frustrations. We can pray it in the name of Christ and live, through and with him, his passion and death. The sentiments of this psalm are constantly being lifted up through the voices of the faithful. The experience of their lives, the sorrows as well as the joys, lead only to one conclusion: "I will praise the name of God with a song; I will magnify him with thanksgiving."

# PSALM 70

*Be pleased, O God, to deliver me.*
*O LORD, make haste to help me!*

༺

This psalm is found incorporated into Psalm 40:13–17. No doubt it was used in a liturgical context, and the author of Psalm 40 saw its relevance to his personal situation and so used it as his own. The lament is typical and, with a bit more freedom, is also incorporated in Psalm 35:24–28.

As a Christian prayer, we would do well to put the emphasis on verse 5: "But I am poor and needy." Verse 4 is ironic, with its statement that those who love God's salvation always say, "God is great!"—the battle cry for present-day terrorists. Perhaps this can be seen as a warning that we must be willing to put our hope in God's deliverance and to pay whatever price this may demand.

# PSALM 71

*O God, from my youth you have taught me,*
*and I still proclaim your wondrous deeds.*

༺

This psalm springs forth from the wisdom and the weakness of advanced age. It is a song of confidence, gratitude, encouragement, and hope. There is no great desire for harm to be inflicted upon the psalmist's enemies. He does ask that they may be put to shame and confused but the impression is given that this shame and confusion will come about when they realize how God has increased his honor and comforted him. It is his praise upon the harp and his song upon the lips that will put to shame those who seek him harm.

Just to repeat the psalmist's words in the first six verses is to experience his joy, his confidence, and the righteousness given to him by God. To repeat his last three verses is to join in with him while his soul and his tongue proclaim God's righteous help all the day long. This is the prayer of an old man in which he recalls how even from the very beginning of his life God was his Father. When he says: "It was you who took me from my mother's womb," he is referring to the custom of a father taking the newly born child from the mother and holding the child in his arms as an acknowledgment of his fatherhood. This is why God is his strong refuge and will not cast him off even in his old age. This is why the number of God's deeds of salvation is past his knowledge. From his youth to his old age, God's righteousness has been with him. We should pray this psalm for the elderly.

# PSALM 72

*Blessed be the LORD, the God of Israel,*
*who alone does wondrous things.... May his glory*
*fill the whole earth. Amen and Amen.*

∽

This psalm was originally intended to be sung in the Temple for the anniversary of the king's coronation. It is a wonderful reminder for all those people who hold political authority that righteousness and justice (mentioned four times), especially for the poor and the needy, is a priority. For us this psalm should unpack the meaning of that phrase in the Lord's Prayer, "Thy kingdom come."

67

We are a royal nation and Jesus, of course, is the king. To some extent, we can see the extension of his kingdom even now. It is not limited to one country or any one place on the earth or even to one lifetime: "May he live while the sun endures....May he have dominion from sea to sea." When God's will is done on earth as it is in heaven, even material prosperity will manifest it. We will be delivered from oppression and violence and we will bless ourselves with his name.

BOOK THREE

# PSALMS
# 73 TO 89

# PSALM 73

*Whom have I in heaven but you?...*
*There is nothing on earth that I desire other than you.*

∽

This wisdom psalm is a meditation on the justice of God. It takes up the theme of the Book of Job. How can we reconcile our belief that God is good to the upright, to those who are pure in heart, when we personally experience so much inequality and injustice in the world? We live in a global village, and the mass media is very active in bringing into our homes and our lives the massive tragedies that occur almost daily in the world. It is a scandal to us, literally a stumbling stone, to see the prosperity of the arrogant and the wicked. They wear their pride as if it were a necklace. Their bodies are sound and sleek, and their eyes are bulging with fatness. Because of their wealth, they receive the praise of others, God is blasphemed, and his providence is questioned.

For the psalmist, the answer came in a sudden grace when he entered the Temple. He had been stupid and ignorant and his soul was embittered, but now by God's goodness he was given to understand where true values lie. Health, wealth, and earthly power are nothing but dreams that are destroyed in a moment. These may fail him, but God is the strength of his heart and there is nothing on earth that he desires but God. It is good to be near God. He makes the Lord his refuge and he so declares this before all.

# PSALM 74

*Rise up, O God, plead your cause.*

∽

It is no wonder that this psalm begins with such a pathetic lament. The memory of a desecration of the Temple, probably occurring around the time of the Maccabees, is fresh in the psalmist's mind. It is as though he had just returned from walking through its ruins. "At the upper entrance they hacked the wooden trellis with axes. And then, with hatchets and hammers, they smashed all its carved work. They set your sanctuary on fire."

The Temple was the psalmist's whole world. Its destruction was a sign that God had left his people. He reminds God of his wonderful deeds of the past, especially in the works of creation. The recent disaster causes his enemies, God's enemies, to scoff. His cause is God's cause.

The Temple for the ancient Jew was a symbol of the entire cosmos. When it was destroyed, that destruction was total. It seemed as though God's work in creation had been put to naught. This is why the psalmist reminds God of his work of creation. As we look about us today and see the destruction that is being wrought in God's world, we have similar feelings. The human race is destroying God's beautiful creation. Environmental disasters, air pollution, wanton misuse of the world's products, man's inhumanity to man, are all evidence of this. "We have met the enemy and he is us!" We should pray this psalm for ourselves and for our world.

# Psalm 75

*I will rejoice forever;*
*I will sing praises to the God of Jacob.*

❦

First, we must see this interesting psalm in its original setting. It is introduced by a group of singers who wish to thank God and to consider his wonderful deeds. They are answered by an oracle or a priest who speaks in the name of God. The theme of this psalm is thus brought out: "Do not boast!" The use of the word *horn* calls for some examination. It had two meanings for the Old Testament Hebrews. It referred to the weapon of a large animal and as such was a symbol of strength, but it could also be hollowed out and used as a drinking vessel. We see both of these meanings in this psalm. "Do not lift up your horn on high" conveys the idea of a triumphant toast before drinking, one in which the proud man extols his own strength. However, the psalmist insists, there is in the hand of the Lord another cup, one that the wicked will be forced to drink. This will be a painful libation, not a boastful one.

We are reminded of the prayer of Jesus in the Garden of Gethsemane, "Father, let this cup pass from me." Jesus had to drink of this cup, which was prepared for the wicked. He had to identify and substitute himself for sinners. Let us pray this psalm with Jesus in mind. He is both the expression of God's glory and love and, at the same time, the holy victim whose love takes upon himself the suffering deserved by us sinners.

# PSALM 76

*Glorious are you, more majestic than
the everlasting mountains.*

∽

This psalm celebrates the ultimate victory of God over all who would oppose him. While it specifies that he is known and recognized in Israel, it refers to his recognition all over the world, especially in the end-times. His dwelling place is in Jerusalem but he is more glorious and majestic than the everlasting mountains. Of special note is verse 10, "Human wrath serves only to praise you, when you bind the last bit of your wrath around you." This means that God turns even evil intentions to his own purposes. He is superior to all earthly kings and princes.

Pray this psalm then for the whole world, the world as we see it today with all of its feeble attempts to challenge God, but also with all of its efforts to honor him. We know that ultimately he will be the victor not only for the entire world but also for each one of us.

# PSALM 77

*In the day of my trouble I seek the Lord.*

∽

You should pray this beautiful and dramatic psalm aloud. It begins, "I cry aloud to God, aloud to God, that he may hear me." God will hear you as you pray for his Church, his world, and for yourself. The next verse, so simple in itself, offers us a profound understanding of our relationship with God. There are times when he seems to withdraw himself, but he does this only to encourage us to seek him. God's steadfast love and his promises will never cease and our own crosses should serve to remind us of that love and those promises. As it was with Jesus, it will be so with us. The cross can lead nowhere else but to the resurrection.

Nothing in nature is so powerful and indeed so frightening as the tumult of the ocean in a storm. This, according to the psalmist, is nothing but the water reacting in fear at the power of God. Remember that the earth trembles and shakes at the clash of thunder and the flash of lightning, but this lightning is an agent of God, and, with it, he lights up the earth. God will lead us in a pathway through the waters as he led the Israelites through the Red Sea.

# PSALM 78

*Tell to the coming generation the glorious deeds
of the LORD, and his might,
and the wonders which he has done.*

This is a lengthy psalm of seventy-two verses. It is addressed to the people in the style of wisdom literature: "Give ear, O my people, to my teaching." The wonderful deeds of God's dealing with his people in the past must be told to the children so that future generations will know of his glory and goodness. There is an obvious reference here to the Passover festival when the youngest child is supposed to ask of the assembly why they are doing the things involved with this meal. The answer given by the elders is the same answer given by the psalm: to declare God's glory and remind them of the wonderful deeds he has done in their behalf. The psalmist goes on to recite in detail the history of God's mercy with his people, yet in spite of all this, they still sinned, and, despite his wonders, they still did not believe.

Even though their hearts were not steadfast, he was compassionate and forgave their iniquity—he restrained his anger. He remembered their weakness when they sinned against him again and again. He led them like sheep and guided them in the wilderness like a flock. Yet, they turned away and acted deceitfully. They suffered because of their disobedience. The wisdom literature clearly teaches that all enemies of God, including we ourselves, fall into the pits that they have dug.

But then the Lord awoke as if from sleep. He chose David, his servant, to be the shepherd of his people. As Christians, we carry this psalm forward into the future and see that it was the off-spring of David, our Lord Jesus, whom God chose to be our shepherd. The ultimate answer to our treachery, our sins, and our weaknesses is that God so loved the world that he gave his only begotten Son and, as St. Paul reminds us, while we were yet in our sin, God loved us and gave himself for us. We should never forget the tender promise in verse 72: "With upright heart he tended them, and guided them with skillful hand." This refers directly to David and then, more directly, to Jesus.

# PSALM 79

*Help us, O God of our salvation,*
*for the glory of your name.*

༼ྊ

Once again, the grief of the psalmist pours forth as he looks upon the ruins of the Temple in Jerusalem. Once again, this prompts him to plead for God's mercy. The emphasis is not on seeking vengeance against those who have destroyed the Temple but on reminding God of the plight of the flock of his pasture. The motive for God's mercy cannot be challenged as it is for the glory of his name. Let us remember, as we pray this psalm, that God seeks vengeance on our enemies by forgiving them—even as we must.

# PSALM 80

*Restore us, O God; let your face shine,*
*that we may be saved!*

༼ྊ

The repeated theme for this psalm is found in verse 3: "Restore us, O God; let your face shine, that we may be saved!" Israel is compared to a vine that God planted and which flourished, even covering the mountains and extending to the very shores of the ocean. We are called to remember that Jesus said he is the vine and we are the branches. There are times when this vine must be pruned. There are times when God must exercise a hard love for our sake. These are the times when the present calamities in our world and the suffering of our Church call for us to join the plea of the psalmist: "Turn again, O God of hosts; look down from heaven, and see; have regard for this vine, the stock which your right hand has planted."

# PSALM 81

*I would feed you with the finest of the wheat,*
*and with honey from the rock I would satisfy you.*

∽

This psalm is beautiful, dramatic, and powerful. Just read it through and experience the drama of God speaking to us, and his longing for us. It was obviously written to celebrate a great feast, possibly the Feast of Tabernacles, a harvest feast. The full orchestra is called to join in his praise. The new moon serves as the calendar for establishing the time of the festival just as we use the new moon to establish the time of our celebration of the resurrection. What a marvelous meditation is provided for us in the simple phrase of verse 5: "I hear a voice I had not known." The voice is that of God who initiates a relationship with us. God always makes the first move. While we are still in our sin, he loves us. He initiated the very fact of our existence from nothing. In him we live and move and have our being.

Instead of the psalmist reminding God of his wonderful deeds, in this psalm God reminds us of those deeds. When he says in verse 7, "I answered you in the secret place of thunder," he is referring to his response to the pleas of his people on Mount Sinai. How easy it would be for us personally to add on to the list of wonderful things that God has done for us as demonstrations of his love. "Open your mouth wide, and I will fill it....I would feed you with the finest of wheat." How easy it is to interpret this in terms of the greatest gift that God gives his people, the eucharistic bread of Jesus Christ. There is a powerful and poignant pleading in the words, "O that my people would listen to me." He promises that if we listen, he will subdue our enemies. Indeed, if we listen to him we will have no enemies because his word speaks of love and forgiveness.

# PSALM 82

*Rise up, O God, judge the earth;*
*for all the nations belong to you!*

Here is an imaginative picture of an idea common in the ancient Near East. The world is governed by a council of gods. The poet, probably a Temple oracle or a priest, sees in a vision God standing up in the midst of the council, chiding them because they do not perform Godlike activities. They do not give justice to the weak or maintain the rights of the afflicted; they have neither knowledge nor understanding. In other words, the gods of the heathens are naught.

You might find it interesting to see how Jesus quotes verse 6 of this psalm in John 10:34. He has been accused of blasphemy by the Jewish authorities: "You, though only a human being, are making yourself God." Jesus replies, "Is it not written in your law, 'I said, you are gods'?" But this is followed by a graphic reminder that they will "die like mortals, and fall like any prince." It is ironic how accurately Jesus himself falls under this very same warning, and how we, his followers, no matter how highly we are exalted by his Spirit, must one day undergo our own passion. We, like him, must also do the works of the Father. These will testify to our being one with God and our being sons and daughters of God.

# PSALM 83

*You alone, whose name is the LORD,*
*are the Most High over all the earth.*

∞

This psalm is a plea to God to deliver Israel from the attacks of her neighbors. To attack God's people is to attack God, and this is the basis of their cry for deliverance. Perhaps this is a psalm that Jesus would not have us pray because it does not conform to the new law preached in his Sermon on the Mount. Yet, in fact, we do pray to be delivered from our enemies. We try, however, to remember that our enemies are also beloved of God.

There is a remarkable redeeming feature to be found in verse 16: "Fill their faces with shame, so that they may seek your name, O LORD." This is a circumlocution for saying that they might seek God himself. We can also interpret verse 18 as a prayer that God's enemies may be brought to know that God alone is the Most High over all the earth.

# PSALM 84

*My soul longs. . .for the courts of the LORD;*
*my heart and my flesh sing for joy to the living God.*

∞

This contemplative poem is one of the most beautiful in the entire Psalter. It is almost superfluous to comment upon it. It is given to us as a beautiful expression of our longing for God and, indeed, it includes in our personal longing the desires of all the members of the Church, and of all the saints and angels in heaven and on earth. Pray this psalm in humble, joyful gratitude.

The Temple is sacramentalized as the presence of God on earth. Even the birds that nest in its walls are protected, as are the men and women who serve in it. One of the most magnificent verses in the entire psalter, these opening lines bring out the true meaning of the Temple and of Jerusalem as its site. Jesus said the day would come when men and women would no longer worship at the Temple but would worship God in spirit and truth. While they are blessed who dwell in God's house forever singing his praise, blessed indeed are those whose strength is in God, who do not dwell under his physical roof but in whose hearts are the highways to Zion. No matter where they are, they bring with them blessings as they go from strength to strength. To pray this psalm is to join the ranks of such men and women!

# PSALM 85

*Faithfulness will spring up from the ground,
and righteousness will look down from the sky.*

∽

This is, at the same time, a psalm of thanksgiving and a psalm of plea. Reminding God of his past favors is simply the means by which the psalmist reassures himself of those favors. The results of this memorial are found in verse 7: "Show us your steadfast love, O LORD, and grant us your salvation." Verses 8 to 13 are God's response given through a priest or prophet. Pray these words and apply them to yourself, "Let me hear what God the LORD will speak." Look for his salvation. Then watch steadfast love and faithfulness meeting, and righteousness and peace kissing each other. Yes, the Lord will give to us what is good and righteousness will go before him. Traditionally this is psalm is considered most appropriate for the Christmas season.

# PSALM 86

*I give thanks to you, O Lord my God, with my whole
heart, and I will glorify your name forever.*

∽

Most of the verses of this psalm are found elsewhere in the Psalter or in the Old Testament. There is little in it that is original. The psalmist uses four different Hebrew names for God, simply translated here as *God* or LORD. Even though its expression is not original, the prayer expressed in this psalm becomes original with each person who prays it. It is not a theological treatise, nor a carefully reasoned argument, but an impassioned plea involving humility, trust, confidence, and gratitude.

All our prayers should begin with humility; that is, an awareness of our need for God. Then we proceed to an acknowledgment of God's goodness, and our love and gratitude for it. Verse 16 deserves some special consideration: "Turn to me and be gracious to me; give your strength to your servant." As Christians, we can truly understand the fullness of this prayer's meaning. God gives his strength to us, first, by giving us his only Son and, second, by sending us his Holy Spirit who is indeed his strength. When we understand this incredible reality, we can see that our prayers must be answered, that God will always pour out his steadfast love upon us, to give us hope and the endurance that it assures.

# PSALM 87

*Glorious things are spoken of you, O city of God.*

This brief psalm begins with an encomium, or expression of high praise, to the city of Jerusalem, beloved by the Lord. It is very common in the Old Testament for the Jews to remind God of his beloved city. Christians should look ahead from here to the teachings of Jesus, where he tells us that the time will come and is now present when God will dwell, not in Jerusalem, but in the midst of his Church. The city of God is now the Church. Verse 3 says, "Glorious things are spoken of you, O city of God." This verse was the inspiration for St. Augustine in writing his great work, *The City of God.*

Among the nations who acknowledge Jerusalem's place is Rahab, a poetic name for Egypt. Foreign nations will envy those who can establish Jerusalem as their place of birth and even the Lord, who keeps a record of such things, will acknowledge this. For Christians the fulfillment of this enviable position is found in their rebirth; that is, in their baptism.

# PSALM 88

*Every day I call upon you, O LORD;*
*I spread out my hands to you.*

∽

This psalm is noted for its despair-like qualities. There does not seem to be even a spark of hope. What can we say then? Should a Christian pray it? Indeed, we should pray this psalm with great fervor. The spark of hope is found in the very fact that we turn to God in prayer in the face of all the disasters that confront the Church and the world. We give voice to all the sufferings of humanity, saying, "Every day I call upon you, O LORD." It is worth noting here that it is the custom in the Divine Office to conclude each psalm with the doxology, "Glory be to the Father and to the Son and to the Holy Spirit." Thus, even the sorrows of the world prompt us to cry up to the heavens and to give glory to God.

# PSALM 89

*Your steadfast love is established forever;*
*your faithfulness is as firm as the heavens.*

ॐ

This is a powerful psalm of 52 verses. It ends with the doxology that points out the conclusion to Book III of the Psalter. The psalm is sung by the king, who declares himself the son of David and heir to all his promises. The king reminds God of those promises—that David cried out, "You are my Father, my God, and the Rock of my salvation!"and that God responded "Forever I will keep my steadfast love for him, and my covenant with him will stand firm."

This seems, however, to be contradicted by the present state of affairs in which the king is praying. He says, "You have renounced the covenant with your servant: you have defiled his crown in the dust. You have broken through all his walls; you have laid his strongholds in ruins." In verse 30 God warned that if David's children ever forsake his law and violate his statutes, he will punish their transgression with the rod, but he will not remove his steadfast love. He will not violate his covenant. David's line will endure forever.

As Christians, we will pray this psalm as coming from the mouth of Jesus, the Son of David. He has also made kings of us and we too are heirs of the promise made to David. There will be times when the Church suffers for her infidelity and is covered with shame, but the Lord's steadfast love will endure.

# BOOK FOUR

# PSALMS
# 90 TO 106

# PSALM 90

*Let the favor of the Lord our God be upon us,*
*and prosper for us the work of our hands!*

≪∘≫

Many have considered this psalm the crowning jewel of the Psalter. It is a prayer uttered by the entire congregation, and thus an individual can very appropriately pray it in the name of all the faithful. The title of this psalm, given many years after the psalm itself, attributes it to Moses, the man of God. This in itself is a kind of recognition of its specialness. Some commentators consider this actually two psalms, verses 1 to 12, and verses 13 to 17, so one can pray it in that way as well.

The theme is the eternity of God as contrasted with our own mortality. During this brief span of life, the only reasonable conclusion is to live prudently and strive for wisdom. In verse 1, it probably makes more sense to use the word *refuge* instead of *dwelling place*. Verse 3 says, "You turn us back to dust," an obvious reference to Genesis. What a marvelous meditation can be inspired by the words of verse 4: "For a thousand years in your sight are like yesterday when it is past, or like a watch in the night." In verses 5 and 6, we see a dramatic statement of the transitory nature of human life. We are like a dream or like grass that flourishes in the morning and in the evening fades and withers. The beginning of Job 14 says that man born of woman is of a few days and full of trouble. He comes forth like a flower and withers. He flees like a shadow and continues not. To understand the brevity of human life is to touch the very heart of wisdom. Embrace the beautiful prayer of verse 12, "So teach us to count our days that we may gain a wise heart."

Verses 13 to 17 may be considered a separate poem. It can be used as a beautiful morning prayer: "Satisfy us in the morning with your steadfast love." The things that we do, the work of our hands, can be of lasting value only when the favor of God rests upon us.

# PSALM 91

*Under his wings you will find refuge;*
*his faithfulness is a shield and buckler.*

൧

While Psalm 90 may be considered to come from the pen of an old man, this psalm reflects the exuberance of youth. Its theme may be expressed in the words of St. Paul to the Romans: "All things work together for good for those who love God" (8:28). The Lord is a refuge from many things, including disease, demons, and the heat of the noonday sun. The words of verse 11 are quoted by the devil when he tempted Jesus in the wilderness. It is a promise from God to protect his Son and us: "For he will command his angels concerning you to guard you in all your ways. On their hands they will bear you up, so that you will not dash your foot against a stone." For many centuries, this has been a psalm especially beloved by the monastic orders, as monks prayed for perseverance in their vocation. The final three verses are an oracle or prophecy that we should take to heart as given by God to us: "Those who love, me, I will deliver....When they call to me, I will answer them...and honor them....With long life I will satisfy them." What a great satisfaction and a privilege it is to pray these words knowing that Almighty God has given them to us for our own consolation.

# Psalm 92

*You, O Lord, have made me glad by your work;*
*at the works of your hands I sing for joy.*

☙

For centuries, the Levites in the Temple sang this song, probably at the morning and evening times of sacrifice and most probably accompanied by musical instruments. It is a common practice among Christians to pray daily, especially in the morning and the evening. This psalm would be most appropriate at those times. The psalmist takes up the theme of the first psalm of those who are good or evil. The good are like a tree planted in the courts of the Lord that flourishes and gives its fruit in due season and even in old age. People who don't realize the greatness of the works of the Lord are the cause of their own unhappiness. The thoughts of the Lord are very deep and go beyond the superficial inconveniences and distresses of our daily life. It is indeed good to give thanks to the Lord.

# Psalm 93

*Most majestic than the waves of the sea,*
*majestic on high is the Lord!*

☙

Beginning with Psalm 93, we have a collection of hymns of praise continuing from Psalm 95 to 99. As did the ancient Jews, we should pray these psalms on occasions of joyous celebration, both personal and communal. Psalm 93 consists mostly of a triumphal and majestic description of the Lord and his role in the creation myth. The world is established, it shall never be moved, and his throne, situated above the waters over the earth, is even more firmly established. Though the waters beneath thunder and roar with the movement of their mighty waves, they can never touch the Lord who is mightier than they. As he is mighty, so are his house and his decrees.

# PSALM 94

*The LORD has become my stronghold,*
*and my God the rock of my refuge.*

∽

This psalm is a lament, and as in all laments, the wicked have an important role. By "the wicked" we should understand all of the problems—social, political, physical, personal, and communal—that the psalmist experiences. He is realistic in acknowledging them, yet he is convinced that the person whom the Lord chastens is happy. This is the way that the Lord teaches us knowledge. Those who do not know the Lord are fools. Yes, there will be afflictions for those who love the Lord, and at times, they will feel as though their foot is slipping, but knowledge will come to them, and they will see the steadfast love of the Lord holding them up. When the cares of their hearts are many, the consolations of the Lord will cheer their souls.

# PSALM 95

*Let us make a joyful noise
to the rock of our salvation!*

∽

This is a liturgical celebration of joy and gratitude: "Let us make a joyful noise!" We can sing this song in our hearts on behalf of all the Church. The very angels can hear this kind of noise. The Lord is God and we are his people. In verses 7 to 11, we receive a prophecy from the priests of the Temple, together with a warning: "Do not harden your hearts." The author of the Letter to the Hebrews quotes these verses as a warning for us to hold fast our confidence in Christ. We should exhort each other every day that none of us may be hardened by the deceitfulness of sin but will hold firm our confidence in Christ. The very recitation of this psalm will serve to increase our confidence and strengthen our faith.

# PSALM 96

*Sing to the LORD, bless his name;
tell of his salvation from day to day.*

∽

In this hymn of praise, the whole earth is invited to join in and give glory to God. "Sing to the LORD all the earth!" The very earth that God has created tells of his salvation and declares his glory. The Lord is great, far greater than the false gods, which worldly people prefer over him in their worship of wealth and power. Give him the glory that his name deserves, and take your cue from all creation to join in with the worship of the heavens, the oceans, the fields, and the very trees of the woods. He will judge the world with his righteousness and the peoples with his truth!

# PSALM 97

*Rejoice in the LORD, O you righteous,
and give thanks to his holy name!*

∽

God's kingship is celebrated in this hymn of praise. God rules over the earth, the heavens proclaim his righteousness, and he governs his people who hear this proclamation. If God is in his heaven, and all is well with the world, it is because of his judgments. Light dawns for the righteous only if we understand our place in this kingdom, our dominion of the earth under God and our responsibility to care for it. We can rejoice in the Lord only by responding to his rule, because the Lord loves those who hate evil and preserves the lives of his saints. The sentiments expressed here are further developed by St. Paul in his Letter to the Romans: "Let love be genuine; hate what is evil, hold fast to what is good; love one another with mutual affection; outdo one another in showing honor. Do not lag in zeal, be ardent in spirit, serve the Lord" (Rom 12:9–11).

# PSALM 98

*Make a joyful noise to the LORD, all the earth;*
*break forth into joyous song and sing praises.*

∽

Although the verbs in this hymn of praise are in the past tense, the thrust of its meaning is in the future. It resembles the sentiments expressed in second Isaiah. God's right hand and his holy arm are responsible for our new song because of the marvelous things he has done. Not only has he remembered his steadfast love and faithfulness to the house of Israel, but also the whole earth has seen it and makes a joyful noise to the Lord. Verse 9 calls us to give this psalm an eschatological interpretation; that is, it refers to the full accomplishment of God's kingdom at the end of the world. We rejoice because we know that the Lord will judge the world with righteousness. When we pray this psalm, we find ourselves in the extraordinary position of allowing the future to influence us in the present. This is because of our confidence and trust in God's loving kindness. We know that his promises will be fulfilled and that he will come in glory.

# PSALM 99

*Extol the LORD our God...*
*for the LORD our God is holy.*

∽

This is clearly a liturgical psalm, probably used at the celebration of the anniversary of the king's coronation in the Temple. Many of the psalms originated in a liturgical context. When the Babylonians destroyed the Temple in the sixth century BC, many elements of the liturgy, particularly those expressed in the psalms, were spread throughout the country into the synagogues. Thus, psalms that expressed national events, celebrations, or tragedies became local and even personal prayers. Yet they still maintained their communal and national orientation.

This psalm centers upon God sitting in the holy place upon the wings of the cherubim in the Temple over the ark of the covenant. At the same time, this is seen as God's place enthroned over the waters above the earth. Thus, he sits enthroned upon the cherubim while the peoples tremble and the earth quakes. "The peoples" refers to the Gentiles. Notice how often the psalmists include the non-Jews as participants in their worship of God. This is something in which Christians historically have been very deficient. They were often more interested in trying to exclude other Christians or non-Christians from their worship. I hope that in our day, with our interest in ecumenism, we can learn something from the ancient Hebrews.

No doubt, at least two groups in the Temple recited this psalm. The refrain or antiphon, "Holy is he," was probably recited by a chorus or by the people attending, something like the way we sing "Holy, holy, holy" at our eucharistic celebrations. Verse 6 reads, "Moses and Aaron were among his priests." Curiously enough, this is the only place in the Old Testament where Moses is referred to as a priest. He is probably referred to in this way in order to give greater prestige to the priests of the Temple. We know, however, that our Christ is the King of Kings and because of our oneness with him, we are a royal people.

# PSALM 100

*Give thanks to the LORD, bless his name.*

∾

Here is a prayer and a hymn of praise that creates the purity of heart it calls for to recite. God gives us this beautiful prayer through his inspired word to make our own. No matter who we are, what our past is, what our present is—no matter how sinful or holy, how faithful or negligent, we have been—we can take these words given to us by God and praise him with a pure heart, a heart made pure by God's Holy Spirit. This psalm needs no commentary, as it speaks for itself and, indeed, speaks for all of creation. "Make a joyful noise to the LORD all the earth. Worship the LORD with gladness; come into his presence with singing."

# PSALM 101

*I will sing of loyalty and of justice; to you,*
*O LORD, I will sing.*

∾

The loyalty and justice the psalmist sings of is his own. He is even boastful about his integrity of heart. He makes promises that he certainly cannot keep. This psalm is probably part of the liturgy for the coronation of the king and sets forth the expectations that will be put upon him during his reign. The intentions are good, even though somewhat unrealistic. However, is it not true that our reach should exceed our grasp, that we should place before ourselves goals that are worth striving for even if impossible to accomplish? Probably a Christian would be much more comfortable praying, "Lord, be merciful to me, a sinner." Yet at the same time, it is good for us to resolve, in the words of this psalm, to walk with integrity of heart.

Right behavior toward God entails right behavior toward our neighbor. Love and justice imply piety and obedience to God. Religious conduct goes hand in hand with moral behavior. We are called, each in our own way, to share the loyalty and justice of which this prince sings. Once again, we recall the theme of Psalm 1. The king will have about him only those who walk in the way that is blameless. We serve such a king. When we pray this noble psalm, we affirm our citizenship in his kingdom.

# PSALM 102

*Hear my prayer, O LORD; let my cry come to you.*

⁓

This is yet another psalm of lamentation. In its structure and its content, it can be compared to Psalm 22, which Jesus prayed on the cross. It is legitimate to ask why there are so many lamentation psalms. If at any given time we were able to examine all the prayers being offered to the deity, we would see that the vast majority of them are what we call "lamentations." They are appeals to God for mercy, justice, deliverance from enemies, relief from sicknesses, and so on. They start by calling upon the name of God, then ask his help for some particular distress, and, more often than not, make a promise or vow that would be fulfilled when the petition was answered. This was understood as something would be pleasing to God. Often too, if the person's faith was deep enough, he or she would thank God in advance, as it were, for answering the prayer. This is the structure of the lamentation psalms and it can be seen clearly in this one.

Included in this psalm are the fragments of a hymn of praise. Verses 12 to 22 are parts of that hymn, as are verses 25 to 28. These latter verses are quoted in the Letter to the Hebrews 1:10. This is done in what we refer to as an "accommodated" sense. It is not used in its literal sense but is almost a poetic application. We are permitted to make such poetic applications to ourselves when we pray the psalms.

# Psalm 103

*The LORD is merciful and gracious,*
*slow to anger and abounding in steadfast love.*

∽

We should pray this psalm whenever we feel gratitude for a particular blessing from God. It is a prayer from the whole person: "Bless the LORD, O my soul, and all that is within me." It can be prayed any time, of course, because there are always blessings from God for which we are grateful. But even when we do not feel gratitude, we know we should have it. This psalm, through the inspiration of the Holy Spirit, places in our hearts and on our lips the right words to express that gratitude.

The poetic expression of this prayer is powerful and beautiful. As far as the heavens are above the earth, so great is God's love, and as far as the east is from the west, so far does he remove our sins from us. He is our father; we are his children. The imagery used to express his paternal benevolence is the same as that used by

Jesus when he expressed the Father's care for us by reminding us of his loving concern for the flowers of the field.

In most of the psalms, there is no concept of an afterlife in heaven. The teaching of eternal life in God's presence developed only after many centuries of reflection and faith in his loving mercy. It is hard to prescind from this teaching especially when we pray psalms like this. The psalmist says that our days are like grass. The wind passes over it (probably referring to the hot winds of the summer coming from the desert), the grass is gone, and its place knows it no more. Yet, he insists, the steadfast love of the Lord is from everlasting to everlasting upon those who fear him. In the first instance, this refers to progeny, but it is a small step from this to a belief in eternal life such as Jesus taught. The psalm ends with a beautiful hymn of praise.

# PSALM 104

*O LORD, how manifold are your works!*
*In wisdom you have made them all.*

ॐ

This beautiful psalm begins with the creation of the heavens. It is described more poetically and more mythologically than in the creation accounts of Genesis. In contrast to the pagan idea of the elements of nature being gods, here the elements of nature are servants of the Lord. He makes the winds his messengers, and fire and flame are his ministers. The earth appears at his beckoning, coming forth from the chaotic waters. Then follows the creation of the animals and plants, with wine to gladden our heart and oil to make our face shine. The Lord creates the passing of the days and seasons. He is even responsible for the movement and activities of animals—also of people as they go forth to work each morning and labor until the evening. Leviathan—in mythology, a monster of the abyss—is nothing but a plaything for God.

In verse 28, we are told that God opens his hand to give food to all who need it and fills them with good things. Christians customarily use this verse or similar words in their prayer of grace before meals. Then, to culminate his creative activity, God sends forth his Spirit and renews the face of the earth. These verses form the basis of the Church's official prayer to the Holy Spirit. We should join the psalmist in his meditative reflections on creation and on God's continuing providence. We pray with him, "May our meditations be pleasing to him for we rejoice in the LORD."

The same author who wrote Psalm 103 probably wrote this psalm. It bears striking similarities to an ancient hymn to the sun god Aton coming from fourteenth century BC Egypt. If it is actually taken from the hymn to Aton, perhaps we can view it as an early attempt at ecumenism. The psalmist felt free to allow a prayer from another religion to enhance his own understanding and his own expression of his worship of God.

# PSALM 105

*Sing to the LORD, sing praises to him;*
*tell of all his wonderful works.*

∽

Israel's relationship with God is a personal one. It is only later in the history of the country that the Israelites focused their attention on creation theology; that is, on God as the Creator of heaven and earth. For them, God is the God of their nation, the God who dealt personally with their ancestors and with them, the God of Abraham, Isaac, and Jacob. He is not the abstract God of the theologians but the concrete personal God of his chosen people.

This psalm recapitulates the wonderful and mighty deeds that God has performed in the history of his people. As Christians, we consider ourselves to be his people. We are the heirs of Abraham, and the inheritance of the Promised Land is ours as our heavenly kingdom. Therefore, the mighty deeds enumerated in this psalm are wonderful works that God has done for us personally, as well as for the Israelites of old. The joyful summons to praise and thanksgiving in the opening verses calls to us to pray this psalm in the name of the Israelites, in the name of the Church, and, indeed, in the name of all the children of God.

We are invited to pray always, to seek the Lord and his strength, to seek his presence continually! One of the ways the Church does this is through her continuous prayer in the Divine Office or Liturgy of the Hours, which consists mostly of the psalms. The account of God's wonderful deeds taken from the books of Genesis and Exodus is given as a reminder of God's covenant with his people. This is emphasized and repeated in the final verses, which remind us that God led forth his people with joy to the end that they should keep his statutes and observe his laws.

# PSALM 106

*Blessed be the LORD, the God of Israel, from
everlasting to everlasting. And let all the people say,
"Amen." Praise the LORD!*

∽

Psalm 106 is to be seen as a continuation of the theme from the
previous psalm. However, the emphasis now is not on the specific
wonderful deeds of God for his people but rather on the unfortunate response of his people to those deeds. Time and time again,
they sinned against the Lord. A detailed recitation of these sins,
taken from the books of the Torah, begins in verse 6. The psalmist
identifies with the nation and her sins in a kind of collective sense
of guilt. But as often as the people sinned, God forgave them.

In our own prayer and reflections, we should extend the
themes of this psalm into the Christian era. If there is a collective
sense of guilt, then we should reflect on the ways in which the
members of God's people, the Church, have sinned against him.
Probably this has never been as catastrophically manifested as in
our present age, an age of mass destruction, genocide, and international injustices. The Church exists in her people, and it is her
people who are responsible for perpetrating or passively allowing
these evils. Again and again, we have to beseech the Lord for his
mercy. "Save us, O LORD our God…that we may give thanks to
your holy name….And let all the people say, 'Amen!'"

# BOOK FIVE

# PSALMS
# 107 TO 150

# PSALM 107

*Let those who are wise give heed to these things,*
*and consider the steadfast love of the LORD.*

∽

This is a thanksgiving psalm. It was probably sung by pilgrims who came to the Temple to celebrate a feast. They gave thanks to God for delivering them from various dangers. Everyone is called to give thanks, and this is followed by special thanksgiving for a list of particular deliverances. Therefore, desert travelers thanked the Lord, as did those freed from prison, those healed from sickness, and those who had traveled by sea. Note especially the dramatic, poetic expression of the last group of pilgrims in verses 23 to 30. A common refrain varies slightly for each occasion: "Let them thank the LORD for his steadfast love." How easy for us to join in this hymn of thanksgiving. We could even add our own list of particular things to be grateful for and conclude each of them with the same refrain. We should also remember to be grateful, not only for the things God does for us personally, but for the things he does for everyone. In this way, even if we are undergoing afflictions, we can be aware of the good things that others are experiencing, and that there are always such good things occurring.

# PSALM 108

*Awake my soul! Awake, O harp and lyre!*
*I will awake the dawn.*

∞

This is a liturgical song and has to do with the ark of the covenant in its accustomed role of leading the armies of Israel into battle. It is entirely made up of segments from Psalms 57 and 60. The ark no longer leads the army into battle—"You do not go out, O God, with our armies"—either because Israel is out of God's favor or because the ark no longer resides in the holy of holies. The psalmist sees the true dwelling place of God as above the heavens where his steadfast love is great. His own heart is steadfast just as God's love is, and he proclaims this by offering this psalm in the morning, accompanied by a harp and a lyre.

We are created in the image and likeness of God. Christ has refreshed and restored that image with his blood, and so we are capable of loving with the same steadfast love of our faithful God. God's love for his people is the same as God's love for any individual person. Our prayer is never isolated, and when the exalted right hand of God delivers the psalmist, he delivers the entire nation. We need not fear our foes, physical or spiritual, because with God we shall do valiantly.

# Psalm 109

*Help me, O Lord my God!*
*Save me according to your steadfast love.*

∽

This is a cursing psalm of the first order and should probably be omitted from the roster of Christian prayers. Some explanation, however, might at least be helpful. The curses used here are traditional and found in most of the religions of the time. The psalmist apparently believed that love for others should be his normal attitude as he expresses in verses 4 and 5. His later violent and repellent language seems to be inspired as a countercurse to offset the black magic curses of his enemies. Notice, however, that while he seems to be enlisting the aid of God to cause them harm, the real cause of harm is to be their own actions. This is often expressed in other psalms in the words, "Let them fall into the pit which they themselves have dug." Frequently we are the cause of our own miseries. Therefore, while this psalm is not an appropriate prayer for Christians or, in fact, for anyone, this particular idea can serve as a helpful meditation on the fruits of our own sins.

# Psalm 110

*The Lord is at your right hand.*

∽

This is a royal psalm probably used for the coronation of the king. It was very popular among the ancient rabbis and was considered a prophecy given by King David in honor of the Messiah who is to come. This is apparent in its frequent usage in the New Testament to refer to Jesus (Matt 22:44; Acts 2:34; Eph 1:20; Heb 1:3, 13).

The new king is also to be a priest as was Melchizedek of old, the priest-king of Jerusalem (Gen 14). We should pray this psalm in the light of the words that Jesus said to Pilate, "You have said it! I am a king!" It is also an occasion for us to reflect upon our own personal role as prophets, members of a royal priesthood and a kingly nation. This psalm is used powerfully by the author of the Letter to the Hebrews. Jesus reflects the glory of the Father and bears the very stamp of his divine nature, not only by his role in creation but also by sustaining the universe in being. The text of the final verse is corrupt, and the translations vary considerably. It's impossible for any realistic interpretation and so leads us in the direction of an allegorical interpretation.

# PSALM 111

*I will give thanks to the LORD with my whole heart.*

∽

This is an acrostic wisdom psalm. In the original Hebrew, it had twenty-two verses, each beginning with a different letter of the alphabet. It was sung by an individual for the congregation at a Temple festival. "Praise the LORD!"—the first verse—is actually the translation of the word *hallelujah*. To study the works of the Lord means to search them out, to meditate on them, to see them in the context of our own lives. Here the "works of the LORD" refers primarily to his dealings with his people in delivering them from Egypt and bringing them to the Promised Land. For us, the works of the Lord are also his ways of dealing with us through his goodness, the sacraments, the Church, and the death and resurrection of Christ. We are called to meditate on these things and on all the personal blessings we receive from God.

Verse 5 says, "He provides food for those who fear him." The food that we receive from God is, of course, the Eucharist. The fear we should have for the Lord is really reverence and awe: not the abject fear of a slave, but the respect of a son or daughter. This fear is the beginning of wisdom and also its high point. It is the fruit of those who study the works of God's hands and brings about a good understanding.

# PSALM 112

*Happy are those who fear the LORD.*

༆

This psalm also begins with "hallelujah," or "Praise the LORD," and again extols those who fear the Lord. A result of this fear, or reverence, is a delight in God's commands. To the psalmist, true immortality was seen through the endurance of one's descendents, but the Christian sees it in eternal life. Wealth and riches were also seen as a reward for honoring God, but the Christian sees real wealth and riches as treasures stored in heaven as Jesus promised. For us, God himself is the reward. The light that rises in the darkness is Jesus Christ, who is the light of the world. The man who fears God shares his riches with the poor. His horn can refer to his cup, which is overflowing in abundance, or it can refer to his strength, which is like that of the ox.

# PSALM 113

*Who is like the LORD our God...*
*who looks down on the heavens and the earth?*

This is another hallelujah psalm and belongs to that group of psalms (113–18) that Jewish liturgical tradition prescribed for the Passover feast. It is an uplifting experience for us to pray this psalm at any time because its sentiments are always valid, even in times of sadness or distress. Indeed, God is to be praised from the rising of the sun to its setting. The Lord is pictured as sitting upon his throne, which is above the heavens. He lifts up the distressed from the dust. He did this by creating them in the first place, but he does it again by re-creating them in his image through Christ at their baptism and as often as they receive his food in the Eucharist.

# PSALM 114

*Tremble, O earth, at the presence of the LORD...*
*who turns rock into a pool of water,*
*the flint into a spring of water.*

∽

This hymn of praise is a joyful, almost playful tribute to God's loving-kindness in creating the nation of Israel: the sea looked and fled, the Jordan turned back, the mountains skipped like rams and the hills like lambs. These, of course, are references to the parting of the Red Sea and the Jordan, and to the trembling of the earth at the presence of God on Mount Sinai. God turned the rock into a pool for Moses and the parched Israelites in the desert.

This psalm may have been written for use in celebrating the feast of Passover. But the psalmist is not simply telling a story of God's past benevolence but is vividly describing an activity of God that has the characteristics of a living and present event. It is important for us to remember that this is also a recapitulation of our own past; that is, these are the wonderful deeds that God has done for *us*. In addition, with the coming of Jesus, we can add many, even more wonderful deeds. So the psalmist speaks, not only of the time of Moses, but of the present, which is the time of the Christ and of his followers who make this psalm and these events their own.

# PSALM 115

*We will bless the LORD from this time on
and forevermore.*

∽

This is clearly a cultic or liturgical psalm. The verses alternated between a choir and a soloist, or perhaps a priest. It is one of those psalms that was sung by the Jews after the Passover supper. No doubt, Jesus and his disciples sang this psalm just before they went out to the garden of Gethsemane. It would seem that the psalmist had experienced some vindictiveness on the part of the pagans against the religion of Israel, and he is using this occasion to get back at them. According to him, the pagans worship wood and stone, which cannot possibly respond to them. These idols, as those who worship them, are incapable of any rational speech or of seeing things as they really are. What are idols made of silver and gold in comparison with God who is in the heavens?

The psalmist calls upon the entire nation, the house of Israel, to praise God. Then he calls specifically on the priests, the House of Aaron, to offer praise. We should feel ourselves included in this summons to praise God, and the words of this psalm can become our words. The idols of silver and gold are any works of human hands that are preferred before God. It is in God alone that our souls will find rest. Those who go down to Sheol cannot praise God. At this stage of development, the notion of eternal life lacked any clarity. It was only at the later stages of Israel's theological development, shortly before the time of Christ, that the afterlife was seen as being in the presence of God and praising him. For us, it is very clear that we shall join in the joyful singing of the choirs of heaven declaring the glories of God.

# PSALM 116

*What shall I return to the LORD
for all his bounty to me?*

∽

This is a hymn of thanksgiving to God who has delivered the singer from a serious physical illness. It begins with a frank, open, and honest avowal of the psalmist's love for God: "I love the LORD, because he has heard my voice." It is spoken to the congregation because the psalmist has come to the Temple to "pay his vows," vows he made in his illness and now fulfills because he is healed. Things had been bad and the snares of death had surrounded him. But the Lord is gracious and merciful and delivered him. He did not lose faith even in the worst of his sufferings, and here he is now, walking in procession into the Temple, singing his praises of God.

Verse 15 is worth singling out: "Precious in the sight of the LORD is the death of his faithful ones." Its literal meaning probably is that God rarely allows those who love him to die young. Obviously everybody dies, even the saints. It is easy to see how this way of thinking is developing into the teaching received by Jesus that Sheol is more than a place of shadows and darkness but, for those who love the Lord, a place of light, refreshment, and peace.

# PSALM 117

*Praise the LORD!*

∽

This brief but beautiful psalm is a doxology, words of praise. It begins with the Hebrew word *hallelujah*, which is, as we said before, translated as "Praise the LORD." God's steadfast love and his faithfulness are probably the most common themes in the entire Psalter. We should memorize this psalm and let it arise from grateful hearts throughout our day. This psalm is claimed by some to have originally been the conclusion to Psalm 116 and by others to have been the beginning of Psalm 118. However, it stands by itself as a very powerful summons to all nations to praise the Lord. We should understand "all nations" as referring to the present times as well as the future. We answer this summons today by making this prayer our own.

# PSALM 118

*O give thanks to the LORD, for he is good;*
*his steadfast love endures forever!*

∾

This is a royal, liturgical psalm sung by the king, the priests, and the faithful: the House of Israel, the House of Aaron, and those who fear the Lord. The very words of the psalm describe the procession of the king and his followers through the Temple gates. They stop and intone their petition, "Open to me the gates of righteousness." The priests respond, "This is the gate of the LORD; the righteous shall enter through it."

The first four verses give us an antiphon, a refrain, a sort of mantra that we can make our own and carry throughout the day: "His steadfast love endures forever." We can say this in our distress, in our triumphs, in our rejections, and in our deliverances. The Lord may chasten us sorely, but every day is the day of the Lord and it is marvelous in our eyes.

Verse 22 applies directly to Christ. In the Synoptic Gospels, he is called the rejected stone that is now the foundation of God's Temple. So in a literal sense, the king recited this hymn; in an allegorical sense, it is Christ who sings it; and in the moral sense, it is we who offer this praise to God. It is our festival procession in which we approach the very throne of God with praise in our mouths.

# PSALM 119

*I run the way of your commandments,*
*for you enlarge my understanding.*

✌

This psalm is a profound meditation on the Law of God. The Law, or the Torah, is not seen here in a legalistic sense. This is clear in the psalm's use of synonyms. Ten words are used as substitutes for *law*, including *testimonies, ways, precepts, statutes, commandments, word,* and sometimes *promise.* This is the longest psalm in the Psalter, and God is addressed or referred to in every one of its 176 verses. In all but seven verses, there is a specific reference to the Law or one of its synonyms.

Obviously, this is a wisdom psalm, which can be clearly seen in its structure. The psalm has twenty-two stanzas, one for each letter of the Hebrew alphabet. Each stanza has eight verses and, in any given stanza, each verse begins with the same sequential letter of the alphabet. Thus, it's the equivalent of every verse in the first stanza beginning with the letter A; in the second stanza, the letter B, and so on. It is possible that by using the alphabet in this way, the psalmist intended to express the idea that the Law said every possible thing that words can say about God and our relationship to him. This psalm also gives us the greatest example of the use of parallelism in Hebrew poetry: the second part of each verse repeats or complements the first part in some way. This can be seen in virtually every verse.

It is worth noting that the psalmist hardly ever refers to what we usually call the moral law, the Temple, Temple ceremonies and Jewish ritual, or the prophetic element in the Jewish tradition. The only sacrifice that he mentions is his own offering of praise

(v. 108). The psalm is a great hymn of praise to the Law. It also includes elements of the lamentation. In verse 21, the psalmist speaks of the insolent; in verse 52, of the godless; and in 115, of the evildoers. He makes it clear that not all his contemporaries share his sentiments, and there are frequent allusions to persecution, scorn, and contempt. He never loses faith, however, and confidently and consistently trusts that his salvation will come from the Lord and that the Lord will be ready to help him, for he has chosen his precepts. The thinking in this psalm is probably more consistent and repetitious than progressive. It remains for the reader to supply this element in his own meditation on these sage verses. It should be read or meditated on, perhaps only stanza by stanza.

# PSALM 120

*In my distress I cry to the LORD,
that he may answer me.*

∽

Beginning with this psalm, we come to a small collection of fourteen psalms within the Psalter that were recited or sung by the ancient Jews as they went up to Jerusalem on one of the three required annual pilgrimages to the Temple (Passover, Shavuot, and Sukkot). As we pray these psalms today, we should, of course, see ourselves as the Church on pilgrimage, making our way to the new or heavenly Jerusalem.

The distress that *we* experience is our environment, which is so often incompatible with the kingdom of God. Deceit and lies surround us as we see those among whom we live placing material values over the law of God. Sojourning in Meshech or among the tents of Kedar simply means living in a place of barbarians where God is not acknowledged. We must remember as we pray this psalm that we are on the way to the heavenly Jerusalem. We are pilgrims, and prayer is at the heart of our journey.

# PSALM 121

*My help comes from the LORD,*
*who made heaven and earth.*

&#8450;

This pilgrimage song is both beautiful and encouraging. The first verse is often misunderstood. The hills were considered the dwelling places of the pagan fertility gods, and their temples were often built there. So when the psalmist lifts up his eyes to the hills, it is not because he expects to see God there—as is sometimes misinterpreted—but because he knows he cannot receive help from that source. Where then, he asks, can he look for help? The answer is that his help will come, not from pagan deities dwelling on the hills, but from the Creator of the hills and indeed from the Creator of the heavens and the earth.

We should often pray verse 2, which the psalmist probably uttered as he entered the Temple precincts: "My help comes from the LORD, who made heaven and earth." It is a prayer that should always be in our hearts and on our lips. It is the answer to every trial and cross that we are called to bear. It is a response to every blessing and a constant source of help and encouragement for every step of our journey toward the New Jerusalem. We should utter it in good times and bad, as we experience fear or hope, sorrow or joy, peace or conflict, faith or doubt, hope or despair, hatred or love. Allow these words to spring forth in every occasion, knowing that they come from the Holy Spirit, and that they are answered even before they are uttered. Take comfort in them as the Lord intends and realize that he who made heaven and earth holds all things in his hands.

The rest of the psalm is the Temple priest's response to the faith of the pilgrim, a response to *our* faith: We will not stumble nor will our sleep be disturbed because the protector of Israel is with us. He will guard and guide us, protect us from the summer heat and the dangers of the dark nights. He will keep our going out and our coming in, now and forever.

# PSALM 122

*Our feet are standing within your gates,*
*O Jerusalem.*

∽

This is a joyful pilgrim's song, probably uttered when the walls and towers of the city of Jerusalem are first seen after days and possibly even weeks of traveling. The pilgrims recall how happy they were when the pilgrimage to Jerusalem was proposed, and now here they are, standing within its very gates after days or even weeks of arduous traveling. Their prayer now is for the peace of Jerusalem and the good of God's Temple in its midst.

How easy it is for us to make the same prayer for the Church. We are the Church, the Body of Christ, the towers and the walls and even the Temple. We pray for our own peace and good. At the same time, we are conscious that we are praying for a successful conclusion to the journey of our pilgrimage on this earth, to the mansions of heaven where God has prepared a place for us.

# PSALM 123

*Our eyes look to the LORD our God.*

∽

This prayer is very appropriate for a pilgrim to say while going up to Jerusalem. His eyes are lifted up into the distance where his imagination places the holy city on top of a mountain. Even higher, elevated above the clouds, sits enthroned the God of Israel. As a servant is ever attentive to the commands of his master, always watching for the slightest motion of his hands to accompany a command, so does the psalmist watch for the hands of the Lord that he may be humbly submissive to his will.

Possibly the psalmist or the members of his community accompanying him have been suffering at the hands of oppressors of some kind. It does not take a great deal of imagination to apply this to our own situations, at work, at home, or even in a political context.

# PSALM 124

*Our help is in the name of the LORD,*
*who made heaven and earth.*

∽

A strong pulse of emotion comes through in the verses of this psalm. Perhaps this indicates that it refers to incidents that are relatively recent to the psalmist in terms of the experience of Israel.

A rapid series of images follow one another. The Israelites would have been swallowed up alive, swept away by a flood, snared in the trap of a fowler. We can easily make up our own imagery to express the dangers to which we could have fallen in the past recent or otherwise. But now we thank the Lord for rescuing us and repeat the wonderful theme that expresses this: "Our help is in the name of the LORD, who made heaven and earth."

# PSALM 125

*Do good, O LORD, to those who are good.*

∽

There are two groups of people in this psalm, those who are good and upright in their hearts, and those who turn aside upon their crooked ways. The Lord will do good to those who are good, but he will lead away the evildoers. Once again, this expresses a principle seen frequently in the psalms, often expressed by the imagery of one falling into the very trap he himself has set. By this is meant that we are responsible for our own good and for our own evil through our actions, but that all of these are done under the watchful eye, the providence, and the justice of God.

# PSALM 126

*The LORD has done great things for us, and we rejoiced.*

∽

This is a psalm of joyful nostalgia. The nation is probably undergoing one of her many reversals of fortune, and the mind of the psalmist goes back to the times when the Lord restored them. Probably he especially has in mind the restoration after the Babylonian exile. Even the Gentiles made note of God's goodness to Israel. It was like something out of a dream, that shouts of joy followed tears and that seeds sown in weeping would bring forth harvest with joy. As Christians, we often express the same experience in terms of our redemption in Christ. Easter Sunday follows Good Friday. We are never lacking in the virtue of hope. Our crosses, our trials, and our sufferings can actually serve as reminders of God's love and goodness, and his fidelity to his promises.

# PSALM 127

*Unless the LORD builds the house,*
*those who build it labor in vain.*

∽

The theme of this beautiful psalm is taken up in the New Testament by Jesus and by St. Paul: "No one can say 'Jesus is Lord' except by the Holy Spirit" (1 Cor 12:3); and "everyone who hears these words of mine and does not act on them will be like a foolish man who built his house on sand" (Matt 7:26). We are not the means of our own salvation, just as we have not been the means of our own creation. Which one of us can add an inch to our growth by our own power? Who among us can build a house or protect a city unless the Lord builds with us and stands guard by our side?

We need to hear this today, both for our personal lives and for the life of the Church. It can be a great relief for us to realize that the Lord is the source of our life and our strength, and that we are called to turn to him in everything that we do.

Verse 3 says that sons are a gift from the Lord. This seems to be unconnected with the previous verses, but it follows along the traditional lines of a wisdom psalm as an application of the abstract principles stated previously. Children are a part of the Lord's response to our needs in building a house, protecting the city, defending our country, and challenging our enemies. Whatever needs we have, we should realize that the Lord is our strength and our help. Without him we can do nothing, but with him all things are possible. Indeed, we can do all things in Christ.

# Psalm 128

*The LORD bless you from Zion.*

This is in many ways a typical wisdom psalm. Wisdom authors frequently repeat the theme brought to our attention in the first psalm. The fear of the Lord is rewarded by prosperity and happiness. Jesus reminds us that this prosperity is better seen as treasure in heaven. The psalmist reminds us of three material blessings that come in the course of our faithful response to God's law: a fruitful and peaceful enjoyment because of our labors, offspring who will carry on our name, and the prosperity of our community.

Material blessings are blessings indeed, and we pray for them as we pray for our daily bread. They can serve as a sacrament to remind us of the greater blessings God has in store for us.

# PSALM 129

*The LORD is righteous.*

∽

In the past as in the present, those who follow the Lord are aware of the long struggle for survival in an unfriendly world. Yet, despite the many things that stand in the way of our service to the Lord and to one another, we will prevail by God's grace. The imagery of what the psalmist wishes for those who attack Israel is vivid and even painful. Grass on the rooftop that withers before it grows was a common phenomenon of Palestinian houses. It withers in the sun and bears no fruit. It has no place in the abundant harvest blessings.

This is not the kind of prayer that a Christian would offer, but it should stand as a reminder that Jesus has given us a new commandment to pray for one another and especially for our enemies. Evildoers will experience the fruit of their crimes, but God loves us all. Indeed, he gave us his only begotten Son while we were yet in our sins.

# PSALM 130

*I wait for the LORD, my soul waits,*
*and in his word I hope.*

∽

This is one of the most beloved psalms in the entire Psalter. The psalm itself is of a late date and tells nothing of the particular circumstances of its composition. It expresses the deep distress of the psalmist's soul as he waits patiently for the Lord to answer his prayer for forgiveness. He gives three reasons that move him to hope that God will listen to his cry. First, he acknowledges the common weakness of man and that none are free from sin. Second, only God can forgive, and it is by exercising its power that we are moved to fear him as our only source of peace. Third, the psalmist is confident that help from the Lord will come even as morning follows the night. As the poet concludes, his thoughts turn from himself to his people as he urges the entire nation to learn from him. By praying this psalm we prove the validity of his aspiration. We turn his appeal for mercy for his iniquities into our own appeal, thus making it the prayer of all God's people.

# PSALM 131

*I have calmed and quieted my soul.*

This beautiful psalm is the perfect prayer for the contemplative to offer before sitting down for quiet meditation. It seems to be the offering of a very active person who has succeeded in going beyond the flurry of daily activities, who has risen above the turmoil of daily concerns and has been led by God's grace to be at peace and to be still and to know that God is with him. Like a child on its mother's breast, the psalmist has calmed and quieted his soul. His prayer, while deeply personal, reaches out as always to embrace the entire community of God's people. Israel, hope in the Lord.

# PSALM 132

*Let your faithful shout for joy.*

∽

This psalm is immersed in the dramatic history of God dwelling in the midst of his people on the mercy seat over the ark of the covenant. It recalls the events recorded in 2 Samuel 7 in which David expressed his determination to provide the ark with a sanctuary. The two cities mentioned in verse 6 are poetic names for Bethlehem, David's city, and Kiriath-jearim, the place where the ark was kept before David brought it to Jerusalem.

Verse 8, which begins "Rise up, O LORD," refers to the procession in which the priests carried the ark upon their shoulders, followed by the rejoicing crowd, singing and dancing. The ark is finally brought to Jerusalem and set down in the holy of holies, which will be its resting place forever. As long as God dwells there, Israel will be blessed with abundance, with salvation, and with power over her enemies. We can pray this psalm actually rejoicing in the mercies that God has shown his people in the past, and that he will continue to show us in the present, as he dwells in our midst wherever two or three are gathered together in his name.

# PSALM 133

*How very good and pleasant it is when
kindred live together in unity!*

∽

This wisdom psalm was probably part of the Temple liturgy, and its purpose was to instruct its listeners in the value of family life. The family was the heart and soul of Israel. Several families were usually bound together under the leadership of a patriarch or grandfather. This institution suffered when the Jews went into exile or when they emigrated to other lands. It was probably also included among the pilgrimage psalms, so it could be recited by the extended family making its way up to Jerusalem.

The precious oil lavishly poured upon the head invokes the custom of a host anointing the head of his guest with perfumed oil. So lavish is this anointing that the oil pours down upon the guest's beard even to the collar of his robes. The beard of Aaron probably refers to Exodus 30, where Moses is commanded to anoint Aaron and his sons to consecrate them as priests. This beautiful psalm can be read very appropriately during family gatherings.

# PSALM 134

*May the LORD, maker of heaven and earth,
bless you from Zion.*

∽

This little psalm, one of the briefest in the entire Psalter, truly sums up what it is all about. It is a summons to praise and a response to that summons with the blessing. The priests are asked to enter into the holy place to praise the Lord. They respond in verse 3 with a blessing. This is the last of the pilgrimage songs. In my monastery in the dark hours of the night, the monks assemble in the entry of the church while the cantor intones, "Come, bless the LORD, all you servants of the LORD." The community then takes up the psalm and continues to chant it while they enter into their places in the choir for the Night Office. This kind of activity is what the Church is all about. Any member of the Church can pray this psalm, knowing that at any given time there are servants of the Lord lifting up their hands to the holy place and that they are truly blessed by this activity.

# PSALM 135

*Praise the LORD! Praise the*
*name of the LORD.*

༄

This is a liturgical song of praise with a joyous interaction among priests, cantors, singers, probably even dancers and a soloist. Verses 1 and 2 constitute a call to praise. Verses 3 and 4 respond to that call: "Sing to his name, for he is gracious!" Then the soloist takes up the reasons for praise: God is the Lord of all the earth, and among his wonderful deeds are all the activities of nature. Then verses 8 to 12 recite the Lord's personal kindness to, protection of, and providence over his people. This summons forth another cry of praise in verses 13 and 14, followed by a typically prophetic mockery of the pagan idols, and then a call to the entire nation, especially the priestly tribe of Levi, to offer praise to God.

This beautiful hymn of praise easily lends itself to a Christian context. God is to be praised for all his wonderful deeds, in creation and in history. Everything that we do that does not lend itself to this praise is in vain and is as useless as a statue carved of wood.

# PSALM 136

*Give thanks to the God of Heaven,*
*for his steadfast love endures forever.*

This beautiful song of thanksgiving, in typical fashion, thanks and praises God for all his wonderful works, beginning with the works of creation, followed by his help establishing his people in their own land, and finally his goodness to each individual. The second half of each verse is the response of the congregation. How wonderful and how easy it is to pray this psalm as a personal prayer as well as an expression of the whole Church. We can even add on to it, especially at the end, the wonderful works of God as we have seen them in our own lives. His steadfast love does endure forever and continues even today. Everything that is, everything that was, and everything that will be, is the result of God's enduring love.

# PSALM 137

*How could we sing the LORD's song in a foreign land?*

The poignancy of this psalm often obscures its real purpose. It is a cursing psalm. It was written after the Babylonian exile in the

fourth century BC and harkens back to the strong emotional long-
ings that the Israelites had for their homeland. In early Israel, the
curse, like the blessing, was seen as a kind of magic entity that
would produce its effects once it was uttered. In later Israel, when
everything was seen as coming forth from the hands of God, its
painful effects were attributed to God's action.

Babylon is personified as a woman and her "little ones" refers
to all of the Babylonians. How can a Christian take to heart the
cruelty of these verses? First of all, we must admit that we do have
such sentiments. There is nothing unique about the cursing element in this psalm. National propaganda in times of war or the
threat of war promulgates such reactions, and we have all been victims of it. In our pulpits as well as our secular platforms, we have
seen similar sentiments corresponding to these feelings of being
threatened. At such times, Christian unity takes a distant second
place, especially when our enemies are themselves Christians.
Reading this psalm should remind us to listen to the unpopular
voices of our own prophets, who are never lacking at such times
and who remind us of the commandment of love.

# PSALM 138

*You stretch out your hand,*
*and your right hand delivers me.*

∽

The psalmist's words are wholly ours: God's name and God's word
are the most important things in mour reality. In the face of all
opposing beliefs, we come to the temple and bow down before
God in thanksgiving for his steadfast love. The time will come

when God's kingdom will reign over all the earth, and every nation will sing the greatness of his glory. The Lord is mighty yet he has regard for the weak. He is high but does not abandon the lowly. Even when cares and anxieties surround us, the Lord's steadfast love protects and delivers us. He will never forsake the souls he has created.

# Psalm 139

*Where can I go from your spirit?*
*Or where can I flee from your presence?*

It is almost futile to comment on this psalm. To pray it with any understanding at all is to be immersed in the all-pervading providence of a loving God. The simplest and most obvious thing to do is to omit verses 19 to 24. The words of verse 18—"When I am awake, I am still with you" (RSV)—are fitting words with which to end this prayer, because the Christian has been awakened by the words and example of Jesus. Pray this psalm and give yourself freely to its sentiments, knowing that you are united with all God's faithful, even from the ancient past to the unknown future. How precious and how vast is the scope of God's thoughts.

There should really be a kind of comfort in realizing God's intimate knowledge of who we are: our plans, our desires, our very thoughts. It is futile to run from him. Whither can we flee from his presence? Even in the darkness of sleep, he is with us. When we awake, he is with us still. Nothing is beyond the scope of his love and protection.

# PSALM 140

*You are my God; give ear, O LORD,*
*to the voice of my supplications.*

∽

Although the inevitable cursing is found in this psalm, the emphasis is on God's protection. Since the time of Jesus, his Church and her individual members have been the victims of persecution. This is so even today. We can pray this psalm for all who turn to the Lord for deliverance. We can also be reminded that we pray for our enemies, not to curse them, but to seek to love them. As often as we fail in this, we know that the Lord maintains the cause of the afflicted, and that we who persevere in our prayer are, by that very activity, dwelling in his presence.

# PSALM 141

*Let my prayer be counted*
*as incense before you.*

∽

This prayer calls to mind the liturgical sacrifice that was offered in the Temple each evening. The psalmist wants his own personal prayer to be seen by God and accepted even as he accepts the official liturgy of the Temple worship. He asks that God protect him from speaking, doing, or even thinking of evil. Let this psalm remind us, if only by contrast, that for the Christian, speaking or even willfully thinking of revenge is giving in to evil. The Lord is true, and the teachings of Jesus are the highest expression of that truth. Bless, do not curse! Love, do not hate! This is the way the Lord keeps us from the traps that our enemies would set.

# PSALM 142

*Give heed to my cry,*
*for I am brought very low.*

∽

By contrast, instead of cursing our enemies, in this psalm we pray for the righteous, that the Lord will deal bountifully with us by surrounding us with them. Here we are encouraged to speak to the Lord, person to person, as with a friend. We can be strengthened simply by speaking to the Lord in detail. We will be strengthened by the very fact of our communicating with him. We can pour out our complaints before him, knowing that he will strengthen our very souls. The best way to be convinced of this is to do it.

# PSALM 143

*Let me hear of your steadfast love in the morning,*
*for in you I put my trust.*

∽

This psalm comes forth from the soul of a deeply spiritual person, one who has a profound knowledge of himself and of God. The reason he gives for God to answer his petition is that God is faithful and righteous. It is not because of the person's own faith or love, because his spirit faints within him and his heart is appalled. His need for God is a thirst, and he longs for him like parched land longs for water. From what God reveals of himself in the sacred Scriptures, this appeal must touch the very core of his divine love. It is a bold request: "Do not hide your face from me." At the beginning of the day, the psalmist longs to hear of the steadfast love of God and understands that he can do God's will only if God teaches him and leads him in the right pathways. The sentiments in this psalm express in a beautiful way the sentiments of St. Paul: "Whenever I am weak, then I am strong" (2 Cor 12:10). It is God's steadfast love, and no efforts of his own, that will bring him out of trouble and preserve his life.

# PSALM 144

*Bow your heavens, O LORD,
and come down.*

∽

The needs of the world are so great that the person who prays often experiences frustration. It is like a man who has only ten dollars and sees before him, with their hands stretched out, all the starving and needy of the world. What can so little do for so many? Through the inspired Psalter, God himself gives us a prayer that can embrace the needs of the entire world. In this psalm, the Holy Spirit, the Spirit of Christ, offers us words of joy, strength, trust, and hope for the needs of the entire world. This psalm does not need to be commented on. It simply needs to be prayed!

# PSALM 145

*All your works shall give thanks
to you, O LORD.*

∽

As the Psalter draws to a close, we see more and more joyful exuberance and the universal call to thanksgiving, praise, and love. To read, or rather to pray, Psalm 145 is to experience this joy. It sums up in itself the best sentiments of the entire Psalter. Reasons for this praise are given as a summation of God's wonderful deeds in the past, a declaration of his wonderful deeds in the present, and a hopeful prophecy of his wonderful deeds in the future. Let us remember that we are part of that past, present, and future.

# PSALM 146

*Praise the LORD, O my soul!*

∽

Psalms 146 to 150 each begin with a brief phrase that summarizes their content and indeed the content of all the psalms: "Praise the LORD"—*Hallelujah!* Psalm 146 is the first of the hallelujah psalms that conclude the Psalter. The next four are clearly congregational psalms, but this one arises from the meditations of an individual expressing what he has learned personally about the goodness of the Lord. What he has learned, under the inspiration of the Holy Spirit, he teaches us. Therefore, we are called to make this psalm our own personal prayer.

We are dealing personally with the fundamental difference between God and man in terms of resolving the basic problems of human society. The style of this psalm is simple and innocent in its literary form, but the content is of great import. The psalmist offers his prayer to God, not for God's majesty, splendor, or power, as shown in creation and in history, but for his concern with the hungry, the oppressed, the blind, the widow, and the orphan. There is a paradox here because of the psalmist's insistence that it is God, not man, who does these things. Yet we know that God operates through human agency and that we are called to be the means by which God sets the prisoners free, opens the eyes of the blind, and lifts up those who are bowed down. Be careful when you say this prayer. You never know what God's grace will direct you into doing.

# Psalm 147

*Sing to the LORD with thanksgiving;*
*make melody to our God on the lyre.*

∽

This is a liturgical, congregational hymn, and so it is the prayer of the entire Church and, indeed, of the entire world. When we consider the needs of the world as a planet and of the countries of the world as a society, a song of praise to God is seemly. What we see is not a Jerusalem strongly situated and gathering the outcasts of Israel, but a country in danger and threatened by enemies from all sides. We see the brokenhearted and the wounded in Africa and Southeast Asia—indeed, in most parts of the world—uncared for and dying. We see an earth, which is itself in danger of dying because of global pollution, global warming, and weapons of mass destruction. We do not see peace in our borders, nor are our children blessed; rather, we see them being sentenced to death in useless wars. We have polluted our own wells and have sold our souls for wells of oil. Nations are starving instead of being filled with the finest of wheat and when God sends forth his word, it is not heard.

Why then is a song of praise to God so seemly? We praise him because when he created the world, he saw that it was very good. We praise him because he has given us the care of this creation. We praise him because he will give us the strength and the grace that we need to undo the horrors of our own past. We praise him because all creation groans in travail but he has given us the love of Christ; he has given us the victory in Christ; he has given us the power to reach out and claim this victory!

# PSALM 148

*Let them praise the name of the LORD.*

Every created thing is given a voice by this psalm. And this psalm gives us a voice so that we can pray through, in, and with all the things that God has created. His glory is above heaven and earth because he sits enthroned above the waters that surround the earth. According to the creation theology found in the Book of Genesis, we are enthroned over all creation, subject only to God. We are given this power through him who has raised up a horn for his people. We are the people near to him because we are the Body of his Christ through his Holy Spirit. We should find great joy and satisfaction in praying this psalm, which lifts us up to God even as we lift up all creation by giving it a voice.

# PSALM 149

*Sing to the LORD a new song,*
*his praise in the assembly of the faithful.*

∽

This psalm of praise calls upon the entire Church to be glad. It concludes with the all-too-familiar military triumphalism over the enemies of God. But we must remember that in verse 1 we are called to sing a new song to the Lord. We are called to praise his name, not only with dancing and with the timbrel and lyre because of the victory that God has given us. Our two-edged sword does not inflict death because it is love. It is a love, which, first of all, is God himself and then is given to us so that we may wield this two-edged sword by our love for one another. This is indeed the glory for all his faithful ones. Praise the Lord!

# PSALM 150

*Let everything that breathes praise the LORD!*
*Praise the LORD!*

∽

Here we have the full orchestration of God's praise. All of the stops are pulled out; all of the musical instruments give voice to praise him. The trumpets praise him, as do the tambourines; so also the strings and pipes, the "clanging cymbals and the loud clashing cymbals." The dancers praise him, and everything that breathes praises the Lord for his mighty deeds and according to his exceeding greatness. Make yourself a part of this magnificent symphony orchestra and this chorus of singers by praying this psalm with a full and grateful heart.